The Urban Environment:
How It Can Be Improved

THE CHARLES C. MOSKOWITZ LECTURES   NUMBER IX

WILLIAM E. ZISCH

VICE-CHAIRMAN OF THE BOARD
AEROJET-GENERAL CORPORATION

PAUL H. DOUGLAS

CHAIRMAN, NATIONAL COMMISSION ON
URBAN PROBLEMS
PROFESSOR OF ECONOMICS, NEW SCHOOL FOR
SOCIAL RESEARCH

ROBERT C. WEAVER

PRESIDENT, BERNARD M. BARUCH COLLEGE
OF THE CITY UNIVERSITY OF NEW YORK
FORMER SECRETARY OF HOUSING AND
URBAN DEVELOPMENT

The Urban Environment:
How It Can Be Improved

THE CHARLES C. MOSKOWITZ LECTURES
SCHOOL OF COMMERCE
NEW YORK UNIVERSITY

NEW YORK   New York University Press

1969

LONDON   University of London Press Ltd.

FOREWORD

THE CHARLES C. MOSKOWITZ LECTURES are an annual event
of outstanding importance. Held each year in November,
they help to advance public understanding of the issues
that are of major concern to business and to the nation
at large. Established through the generosity of Mr.
Charles C. Moskowitz, a distinguished alumnus of the
School of Commerce and formerly Vice-President-Treasurer and a Director of Loew's, Inc., they have enabled
the School to make a significant contribution to public
discussion and understanding of important issues affecting the American economy and its business enterprises.

The 1968 lecture series was on the overall theme
The Urban Environment: How It Can Be Improved, and
brought to our platform three Americans who are heavily
involved in seeking ways through which our nation may
improve the urban environment. With business, educational, and governmental experience of conspicious com-

v

petence characterizing their backgrounds, they discussed the roles of business and government in overcoming the most stubborn problems facing our urban centers, for example, unemployment, pollution, housing, crime, and so on. Mr. William E. Zisch, Vice-Chairman of the Board and Director of the Aerojet-General Corporation, as well as a leader in the creation of the Watts Manufacturing Company in that ghetto area of Los Angeles, spoke on "The Urban Environment: The Role of Business and the Profit Criterion." Senator Paul H. Douglas, presently returned to the academic world as a Professor at the New School for Social Research but still active in the public sector as Chairman of the National Commission on Urban Problems, spoke on "Jobs: A Key to Improving the Urban Environment." Former Secretary of Housing and Urban Development Robert C. Weaver, who became President of the Bernard Baruch College of the City University of New York in the beginning of 1969, centered his lecture on "The Role of Government in Improving the Urban Environment."

Mr. Zisch opened the lecture series with this challenging statement:

> . . . we face a difficult choice: either we will wake up and attend to these problems at whatever cost— and the cost is bound to be high both in effort and in dollars; or we will witness the still more complete disintegration of the urban environment until it becomes an unending source of crime, violence, riot, disease and danger that will affect all our lives and in the end cost more in suffering and financial loss than the costly remedies we must now prepare ourselves to apply.

He went on to identify three elements as being necessary to a solution of our urban environment problems: (1) national concurrence on the goal; (2) readiness to spend the sums required; and (3) application of the most modern managerial techniques to the problem, that is, the systems-analysis approach. Amplifying, he identified these relevant efforts as the basis for his analysis: (1) the President's Test Program for Job Development to ease the hard-core unemployment problem in five test cities; (2) the establishment and development of the Watts Manufacturing Company in the heart of that Los Angeles ghetto area; and (3) California's application of the systems-analysis approach to such urban problems as waste disposal, transportation, and crime prevention.

Reviewing the five-city test program Mr. Zisch observed, "The most significant proposals and, in my opinion, those providing the best opportunity for lasting solution of the problem *were not the typical on-the-job training type.*" He emphasized that, in his judgment, the higher-cost programs were a better investment because they promised to transform the trainee into a responsible full-time worker and taxpayer.

Vis-à-vis the record of the Watts Manufacturing Company, the speaker noted that, without help from advertising, 5000 applications were received for the several hundred jobs originally available. They convinced him that the desire to work exists among the hard-core unemployed. He added that such people were hired without restrictions, even if they had police records or had never held a job before. Only willingness to work and ability to respond to minimum training were expected.

There were problems. Initial absenteeism was high.
However, the Watts Manufacturing Company is now a
growing concern. Further, Aerojet-General has established two plants in areas of previously severe unemployment—Batesville and Camden, Arkansas—employing
about 1000 persons in each. The objective according to
Mr. Zisch is to establish facilities in rural areas because
this helps prevent migration of the rural unemployed
to already overcrowded urban areas.

In a particularly significant and original series of
observations, Mr. Zisch drew upon his knowledge of the
application of the systems-analysis approach to four important socio-economic projects by aerospace companies
in California. Discussing them, he expressed his firm
belief that the managerial techniques developed to meet
the requirements of the space age could be applied practically to the changing urban environment and the solution of our urban problems if means could be found to
finance such efforts properly. However, he thought, this
would have to be done either on a regional basis or by
the federal government responding to a strong expression
of the national will that our urban problems be solved,
not by police power, but through modern, scientific
means now at our disposal through profit-oriented enterprise.

Mr. Zisch's emphasis on the application of the systems approach to our nation's urban problems seems to
me to have seminal significance. He suggests, at least by
implication, that all aspects of the difficulties facing our
urban centers, unemployment, education, housing, crime,
pollution, and so on, be brought together at the national

(federal) level, either in the form of a new cabinet position or in the form of a coordinating and integrating head
of cabinet rank. In this way, a total view of the urban
environment will be achieved and a total commitment
can be more readily made. At the least, the partial, dis-
parate, and sometimes competing programs of the Labor,
Health Education and Welfare, Housing and Urban
Development, and other departments and agencies of the
federal, state, and local governments can be brought
together into some semblance of systematic attack on our
urban problems. It is a testimonial of no mean magnitude
to Mr. Zisch's perspicacity that President Richard M.
Nixon announced several weeks later the appointment of
Dr. Daniel P. Moynihan as a coordinator of federal
efforts to overcome our urban problems.

Another major point made by the speaker involved
the manner in which public efforts to improve the urban
environment are tied to private, that is, business efforts.
In essence, he maintained that business involvement will
not be effectively enlisted without a real prospect of
business profit, for business functions to make a fair return for its principals or its shareholders. He argued that
it is an axiom in American life that when business (or industry) is offered a profitable venture, it manages to find
solutions to our social problems. He cited the toll roads,
which opened up the wilderness of young America and
the canal routes and the railroads, which were subsidized
by the government but which were developed and managed by private enterprise, all of which expanded our
nation and improved its life. Mr. Zisch cited other examples of governmentally aided activities, for example, air

traffic, overland highway transport, Social Security, insured bank accounts, Medicare, help for dependents of
all ages, and the vast expansion undertaken in the housing field. All these have been equally dependent upon
government support for their initiative and financing. In
short, he pointed out that Americans shy away from
socialism as an ideology, yet they have, as a practical
matter, been socialized by government contract to private
industry for nearly two centuries.

Senator Douglas emphasized employment creation,
that is, jobs, as the essential cure for our urban ills. The
principal thrust of his lecture was that employed people
would be busy in constructive rather than criminal pur-
suits, and the income that they earned would enable
them, out of their own increased purchasing power, to
buttress public efforts to upgrade urban housing and
public services.

From an historical standpoint, Dr. Douglas identified the "agricultural revolution" and the massive migration from farms to metropolitan centers which resulted
from it as the principal source of our most serious urban
problems, those associated with the black ghettos of the
inner cities. Millions of people were displaced by the
mechanization of agriculture to the cities. Of at least
equal importance, however, was the fact that those who
made the move were younger, less educated, less skilled,
and less successful than those who remained on the land.
Being hand rather than machine workers, they were even
more difficult to absorb economically in the city's labor
force than they had been in that of the rural economy.
On top of the foregoing facts, Senator Douglas noted

that the high birth rates of the period between 1945 and
1950 brought into the labor market an added group of
young workers, so that, in his words, "The combination
of the coming of age of boys and girls born in this period
of high net fertility and of internal imigration has therefore enormously increased the number of persons and
particularly young people who must find work in urban
areas. This has resulted in a high rate of unemployment
for the urban young." He noted also that the magnitude
of the unemployment problem among black youths in our
urban centers is understated by the official statistics because the official data fails to count people "who sleep in
alleys, abandoned autos and vacant dilapidated houses."

The upshot, according to the Senator, is that ". . . in
some slum ghettos the rate of unemployment for the
16-17-year-olds may run as high as 40 to 50 percent, and
. . . continue at high rates up to and indeed including
full manhood." He added, "These groups, together with
the boys and girls under 16 whom they influence and
those from 20 to 24 into whose ranks they graduate are
immediately responsible for most of the added disorder
and crime which has broken out in our cities during the
last three years."

In the foregoing context, it is obvious that the creation of jobs for these disadvantaged and dispossessed
youths is of foremost importance. To that end, Senator
Douglas put forward a three-point program, which he
designated as minimal.

First, he called upon the federal, state and local
governments to increase public employment through the
creation of a half-million new jobs for the youth of our

country. He estimated this would cost about $2.5 billion per year. Because all levels of government presently employ 10 million full-time workers (as well as another 1.2 million part-time employees), he thought the addition of a half-million jobs quite reasonable, expressing the conviction that they could be created in our schools, hospitals, highways, parks, waste disposal, and other service activities, so that "our cities would be shining rather than repulsive communities. . . ."

Second, and more specifically, he pointed out that we should not neglect the possibilities offered by the housing program. Noting the enormous volume of housing construction needed in our nation, if we are to achieve what we would consider to be tolerably decent living quarters for almost all Americans, Senator Douglas viewed America's commitment to decent housing for all as the real test of our sincerity in combatting the slums that are at the core of our urban problems. Of course, commitment to a massive program of housing construction means a major expansion of employment in that sector of the economy. However, it would be necessary to insure that a large proportion of the added jobs in construction went to those needing them. According to Senator Douglas, the craft unions in the building trades would have to cooperate, and housing construction would have to be based on a relatively standardized product or set of components, a point which might bring the Senator into some disagreement with those urban planners who deplore the alleged monotony and tastelessness of huge standardized apartment complexes.

Third, as government moved forward to create more

jobs in the public sector and in the construction industry, the private sector should also exercise initiative to create jobs. In this connection, Senator Douglas applauded the efforts of the National Alliance of Businessmen which, under the leadership of Henry Ford II, had pledged itself to absorb 500,000 unemployed by 1971. He added that "Some subsidies should . . . continue to be given as an inducement for private industry to take on the disadvantaged."

Estimating the cost of his three-point program at approximately $5 billion per year, Senator Douglas specified five sources of the required funds: namely, (1) the increase in governmental revenues associated with further growth in the national income; (2) the diversion of a respectable proportion of the funds now devoted to the war in Vietnam, once the scale and intensity of that conflict diminished; (3) the reordering of our national priorities, so that space conquest and supersonic aircraft were given less importance and slum problems more; (4) the plugging of some of the loopholes in our federal tax system; and (5) the levying of a tax, à la Henry George, on the increase of land values in America. And, from another angle, public expenditures associated with relief, riots, crime, and punishment would decline while public revenues would be expanded by the taxes on the increased earnings of our formerly unemployed urban poor. The essence of Senator Douglas' prescription is job creation. His lecture identified the major sources of employment and the funds to create it.

Secretary Weaver, relying on his vast experience in the fields of housing and urban land use, pointed out that there are two basic aspects to government's role in improving the urban environment. "The first relates to the functions that public agencies perform in urban America. The second deals with the allocation of these functions among different levels of government and the relationship among these levels."

Turning to the first aspect, he emphasized that public involvement in urban matters is widely taken for granted, so that much current discussion concentrates upon effecting a partnership between public and private resources and institutions, usually through the mechanism of public subsidies, which makes it possible to achieve social goals and still yield a profit to the private sponsor or investor. Noting that some people emphasized tax incentives, as contrasted with some form of subsidy, Secretary Weaver expressed the firm conviction that the former alone would be inadequate to the achievement of our urban goals and social purposes.

The Secretary rejected the idea that "black capitalism" in the ghettos would, at least in the near future, contribute greatly to the improvement we seek. He rejected the idea that black entrepreneurs could be devloped in time on a sufficient scale to take the lead in the physical reconstruction of ghetto areas. Centuries of discrimination and institutionalized color patterns, both in finance and the building trades, have resulted in a situation where there are few ghetto businessmen who now have the capital, capacity, and experience to compete effectively in the construction (housing) industry. Thus, if construction is delayed while a new segment of entrepreneurship is developed, thousands of nonwhite families will have to wait, perhaps a long time, for better housing.

The Secretary argued that America must use the tools that will provide the maximum volume of housing for low- and moderate-income households as quickly as possible, including the development of effective black entrepreneurship and the encouragement of nonprofit and cooperative sponsors.

The rapid growth of the American population, which is likely to continue to characterize the next few decades, led Secretary Weaver to emphasize even further that America requires an enormous amount of additional housing, and the infrastructure (schools, streets, sewers, electric lines, and so on) associated with it. He spelled out the enormity of the overall challenge by referring to such real constraints as an inadequate supply of trained labor, a periodically inadequate flow of mortgage financing, a lack of sites for subsidized housing, a fragmented building industry, inhibiting zoning and taxation policies, antiquated building codes, inflexible labor union regulations, and governmental red tape. He observed further that these constraints are no greater than those turning on problems of poverty, race, citizen participation, proliferation of local governments, municipal finance, and segregated residential patterns.

Having discussed at some length the functions of the public sector in improving our urban environment, as well as the relationship between the public and private sector, Secretary Weaver turned to the allocation of the public functions between the different levels of government. He pointed out that our country has developed a concept of local initiation, development, and operation —limited by federal program requirements and federal review and evaluation of performance. The local initiation and local operational responsibility prevent the federal bureaucracy from operating and controlling programs (and local government). They also permit the degree of flexibility in operations a large and diversified nation requires. At the same time, federal requirements and standards, as well as federal review of achievements and expenditures, provide protection against local abuses. Our system shares authority and thereby hopes to avoid the excesses and abuses of undivided authority.

Secretary Weaver devoted the final portion of his lecture to the role of the state governments, pointing out that there is a pressing need for state involvement. However, it should not be a sterile injection of another layer of bureaucracy that makes no positive contribution. Rather it should be an involvement that channels resources, on an equitable basis, to urban communities or one that deals with problems which the states are uniquely capable of handling. Because the states have all the powers they have not relinquished either to the federal government or to the local governments, they still retain enormous authority. Also, their number and diversity, as contrasted to a single national government, make them less feared as a source of central control and more flexible in program development.

The Secretary observed that there are a series of crucial roles that the states can and should perform. For example, the states are the units of government that will have to assume responsibility for carrying out any meaningful urban land policy. Also, because local governments are the creatures of the states, the latter have both the authority and responsibility to take steps to modify any state-created government agencies that no longer respond to the needs of an urban society. Other institutional impediments to orderly urban development are zoning, building codes, tenant-landlord relations, and local taxation. In these matters, too, the state has the responsibility and the authority to act. So far, only a few states have done so.

In concluding, Secretary Weaver emphasized even more strongly that the states have a vital role in urban affairs, one which transcends simply serving as an additional link in the bureaucratic line of administration. He argued that, rather than concentrating their talents and great leadership potential upon control or additional supervision of local programs, the states should emphasize developing a role of helping local governments with those urban problems which they cannot deal with alone and from which the federal government is largely precluded by law and tradition.

What are the leading lessons we may derive from the 1968 series of Moskowitz Lectures? These are the ones that were most deeply impressed upon my mind:

1. America must arrange its social, economic, and political priorities so that the leading item on the national agenda is the improvement of its urban centers.

2. The public sector must play a principal part in organizing a national concurrence on this objective. It must also be the principal planning element in our society and the means for marshalling the funds necessary to attain the goal.

3. Although all levels of government have vital roles to play, the critical one is that of the federal government. Indeed, it is the federal government which can most meaningfully encourage the application of the systems

approach to the solution of our urban problems. And the application of the systems approach is a critical element necessary to ultimate success.

4. Improvement of the urban environment will be achieved most rapidly and most efficiently only through the large-scale involvement of business in the effort. And the involvement of the private sector must rest upon a frank recognition of its nature and of the stimulus afforded by the opportunity to earn a profit.

5. Of all aspects of our urban problems, the situation in the slum centers is the most critical. And, having centered on the ghettos and their residents, the most immediate avenues of attack according to our speakers are jobs and housing.

And so, this Foreword concludes with Mr. Zisch's astute opening comment:

> . . . either we will wake up and attend to these problems at whatever cost—and the cost is bound to be high both in effort and dollars; or we will witness the still more complete disintegration of the urban environment until it becomes an unending source of crime, violence, riot, disease and danger that will affect all our lives and in the end cost more in suffering and financial loss than the costly remedies we must now prepare ourselves to apply.

Abraham L. Gitlow
DEAN
SCHOOL OF COMMERCE
NEW YORK UNIVERSITY

January 1969

THE CHARLES C. MOSKOWITZ LECTURES

THE MOSKOWITZ LECTURES have been established through the generosity of a distinguished alumnus of the School of Commerce, Mr. Charles C. Moskowitz of the Class of 1914, who retired after many years as Vice-President-Treasurer and a Director of Loew's, Inc.

In establishing these lectures, it was Mr. Moskowitz' aim to contribute to the understanding of the function of business and its underlying disciplines in society by providing a public forum for the dissemination of enlightened business theories and practices.

The School of Commerce and New York University are deeply grateful to Mr. Moskowitz for his continued interest in, and contribution to, the educational and public service program of his Alma Mater.

This volume is the ninth in the Moskowitz series. The earlier ones were:

February 1961   *Business Survival in the Sixties*
THOMAS F. PATTON

November 1961   *The Challenges Facing Management*
DON G. MITCHELL

November 1962   *Competitive Private Enterprise
Under Government Regulation*
MALCOLM A. MACINTYRE

November 1963   *The Common Market: Friend or
Competitor?*
JESSE W. MARKHAM
CHARLES E. FIERO
HOWARD S. PIQUET

November 1964   *The Forces Influencing the
American Economy*
JULES BACKMAN
MARTIN R. GAINSBRUGH

November 1965   *The American Market of the Future*
ARNO H. JOHNSON
GILBERT E. JONES
DARRELL B. LUCAS

November 1966   *Government Wage-Price Guidelines
in the American Economy*
GEORGE MEANY
ROGER M. BLOUGH
NEIL JACOBY

November 1967   *The Defense Sector in the American
Economy*
JACOB K. JAVITS
CHARLES J. HITCH
ARTHUR F. BURNS

CONTENTS

THE ROLE OF BUSINESS
AND THE PROFIT CRITERION

by William E. Zisch

IT IS PROBABLY most appropriate that we should meet here today in the largest city of America to discuss the problems of urbanization. New York has long been the symbol of the progress—as well as the problems—of our cities.

Cities are a paradoxical phenomenon. They are at one and the same time the acme of a civilization and a continuing new frontier that must be explored and managed if we are to provide a better life for future generations. They are—as any frontier must be—a struggle with an environment of an unknown nature. They are forever in a state of reconstruction and hopefully continuous improvement. This work, like many other human endeavors, goes on spasmodically. Usually we wait too long before tackling pressing problems so that when we get to them they seem insurmountable. That is the situation in which we find ourselves today, a little more than a year away from the 1970's. That is why there is such urgency today in thinking about our urban problems and in devising means for meeting them before they overwhelm us. The totality of these problems is part of what we define as the urban environment. They encompass such factors as population density, housing and transportation, sanitation, public safety, air and water pollution, and the many other aspects of city life which set it apart from country living and the amenities of the suburbs.

The problems of the central city have multiplied as individuals or groups have sought to find individual or group solutions to their relationship to the urban environment. The more fortunate groups have overcome population density and housing, as well as air and water pollution, by removing themselves from the crowded areas of the inner city to the suburbs. They have solved their own transportation problems, after a fashion, by the use of private cars. This solution in turn has been largely responsible for the breakdown of the old mass transit systems (both steam railroad and electric cars) within the city. Problems of sanitation and public safety also are much easier to solve in the suburbs—while within the inner city these services have suffered decay because more and more they have come to serve the less-privileged and the less-demanding sectors of the population.

These are the problems of the urban environment we face today, and, unhappily for most of us, they will have to be solved largely by persons who for the most part live outside the city, but a majority of whom work and earn their living within the city. I say "unhappily for most of us" because we face a difficult choice: either we will wake up and attend to these problems at whatever cost—and the cost is bound to be high both in effort and dollars—or we will witness the still more complete disintegration of the urban environment until it becomes an unending source of crime, violence, riot, disease, and danger that will affect all our lives and in the end cost more in suffering and financial loss than the costly remedies we must now prepare ourselves to apply.

Since World War II we have become aware of the decay of the central city and the cultural dominance of suburbanism. It has been said that where once the urban environment dominated the suburbs, today the suburbs dominate the city. However, this is not entirely true, nor do we wish it to become so. I am confident that the temporary dominance of the suburbs will give way once again to the city when the city is put in order.

We must appreciate that urbanization has been the peril of the human race since urbanization began. The classic writers of ancient Rome tell us of the perils of urban life in the time of the Caesars, and the poet Dante pictured hell as seven circles of urban torture. Jacob Riis, a practical student of tenement life in New York just before the turn of the century, gave us the details in his famous book, *How The Other Half Lives*. In Riis' day, as the title of his classic study indicates, 50 percent of the urban population lived in penury, disease, and crime. Since then, of course, foreign immigration has been drastically reduced, a series of reform administrations have had their impact upon all major cities in

America and the percentage of our citizens to whom slum living is an accepted way of life has gone down significantly.

However, we are still far from achieving *The Promise of American Life* that Herbert Croly wrote about sixty years ago. It is interesting that Croly's classic has been revived in recent years because his words apply to our nation and our problems today as fully as when they were written during the first decade of this century when all seemed well with the United States. Croly wrote of extending economic opportunity to all citizens as we extended the suffrage. He said:

> In a wholesome democracy every male adult [this was before women got the vote] should participate in the ultimate political responsibility (suffrage) partly because of the political danger of refusing participation to the people and partly because of the advantages to be derived from the political union of the whole people.
>
> So a wholesome democracy should seek to guarantee to every male adult [this was before equal opportunity legislation came into being] a certain minimum of economic power and responsibility.
>
> No doubt [he continued], it is easier to confer the suffrage on the people than to make poverty a negligible social factor, *but the difficulty of the task does not make it the less necessary.* . . . Not only does a considerable amount of grinding poverty constitute a grave social danger in a democratic state, but so, in general, does a widespread condition of partial economic privation.

The validity of these observations, made 60 years ago, has been demonstrated to us in the last twenty years. Although through legislation we have widened the suffrage among our citizens, particularly among Negroes, and although both political parties this year urge extension of the right to vote to youths of eighteen, *we have not*, in this unprecedented era of prosperity, proportionately extended the economic reach of these previously disfranchised citizens by providing jobs. Thus, today there is grave danger to our democratic state because of a widespread condition of grinding poverty or partial economic privation among the recently politically liberated in our land. All these problems are part of the urban environment to which I address my remarks.

As we all know, the "other half" of which Jacob Riis wrote had by Franklin D. Roosevelt's time been whittled down to one-third of a nation which he described as "ill-housed, ill-clothed and ill-fed." And this percentage had been further reduced to one-fifth by the time John F. Kennedy came into the presidency. Today the general estimate of poverty, rather generously described as those with a family income of less than $3500, is placed at 10 percent. However, before I go on to my principal theme, I would like you to note the comment of another observer of the American urban scene. Michael Harrington has looked over our land in his book, *The Other America,* and he notes that there is an invisible hand of poverty seldom seen by most of us, who witness only the familiar America celebrated in speeches and advertised on television and in the magazines. This familiar America has the highest mass standard of living the world has ever known. Within that affluent society, however, there is another America, which Harrington estimates at 40 million, but which more conservative analysts put at between 20 and 25 million. They are poor. Many of them are old and ill *and many of them are young and jobless.* These latter are the source of much of the violence that threatens to destroy our cities. They are the major debits—in the cost of crime and its correction—against the high taxes an urban dweller pays.

Later on I propose to give you more detailed statistics on the relationship between population density, low incomes, and the crime and delinquency susceptibilities of the younger age groups. Also I shall describe something of the cost to society of these conditions and some suggestions for remedying them made as the result of a survey conducted by physical scientists in which they applied the exact measurement techniques to crime and delinquency problems that they had been using in aerospace developments.

I intend to emphasize that the solution of our urban environment problems will only come when the American people as a whole develop an effective and united will to meet and solve these problems. It will only come when, further, they are ready to spend public money on them, so that the operations of private business and industry, the necessary immediate agencies of their solution, will be profitable. And largely, I believe, it will come through the application of the techniques we used in building up our ballistic missile systems and the management methods which have made possible the conquest of space in the last decade. Three factors are involved: (1) the concurrence of the American people that this must be done; (2) the readiness of public agencies at all levels

of government to appropriate necessary funds, and (3)
the already demonstrated ability of technologically oriented business and industry to match their knowledge
and their creative purposes to master the most complicated challenge and come up with effective and meaningful solutions.

Critics of our industrial system have not been slow
to point to what they call its moral unreadiness to deal
with the major problems of our society. John Kenneth
Galbraith has been conspicuously one of these. Another
younger and somewhat less-well-known critic is Paul
Goodman, a former hero of the young radicals. Not long
ago, in a speech which he described as a "causerie" before a group of leading American industrialists in Washington, Goodman turned to the problems of urbanism
and said:

> Prima facie, there are parts of urban planning—
> construction, depollution, the logistics of transpor-
> tation—where your talents ought to be particularly
> useful. Unfortunately, it is your companies who have
> oversold the planes and the cars, polluted the air
> and water, and balked at even trivial remedies, so
> that I do not see how you can be morally trusted
> with the job.

However much it annoys—even angers—the business
community to be told such things by such a critic as
Goodman, I think there is something to what he says.
There is no question but that business and industry—in
the past and the present—have contributed to the problems we face. However, I think also that business and
industry on the whole have contributed much more to

humanity's betterment than to its demeanment. Also I think that on the whole business and industry are prepared today to do their full share to find a viable solution of the twin problems of unemployment and poverty. I reject outright the fact that businessmen or industrialists are somehow more immoral than the rest of our population, or that they are less concerned with orderly progress toward a practical utopia.

But to get back to the poor and jobless about whom we must concern ourselves. They are the ones who inhabit the miserable housing of the central areas of our cities, where they are increasingly isolated from contact with or the sight of anybody else—except through the lurid headlines of their tabloid newspapers or the flickering tubes of their credit-bought TV sets. They are the failures, the unskilled, the minorities—white and black and brown—who live "across the tracks" where they have always been.

There is another factor. They are there—but hardly anyone else is. The rest of the population—including the skilled and semiskilled—are in their comfortable lodgings in or about the suburbs. The central city is gray and foreboding. The other areas are green and reasonably cheerful.

There is still another factor. In other days, the ratio of the poor and the unskilled in our society was relatively high. Today, the percentage of these disadvantaged people is at its lowest, whereas the affluent or relatively affluent are both more numerous and more visible—and mostly out of town. This contrast too, is part of the Urban Environment.

As we all know, there has been much progress through the years. The ever-decreasing ratio of the poor and the unemployed, of the unskilled jobless, gives hope that "the promise of American life" is being fulfilled. However, 10 percent is too high a ratio in the affluent age that this nation has been enjoying for nearly three decades.

The drive must be for greater progress, and the leadership in this effort must be taken by business and industry, motivated, as they have always been in the past, by expectation of a reasonable profit for providing needed products and services to the whole community.

We may not be on the brink of conquest of our urban ills, but the fact that we are aware of them as never before is encouraging. They are of concern to governments at all levels. They are part of the ubiquitous cry for law and order and justice. They are part of the programs which local communities, states, regional authorities and the federal government itself are proposing for the years ahead. They are being analyzed by social scientists and probed by the best business minds of the nation. The National Alliance of Businessmen and the Urban Coalition, headed respectively by Henry Ford II and John W. Gardner, our former Secretary of Health, Education and Welfare, are characteristic of the interest in high places which our urban problems have elicited. Now, with the national election over, we can have hope at least that a real beginning will be made. I say this because I believe strongly that this never was a partisan issue.

President-elect Nixon has repeatedly pledged to expand the participation of private enterprise to coping

with our social problems. The objectives will be to provide jobs for the unemployed, train the unskilled, build
more housing and improve health care. The Johnson administration also invoked these goals and sought as-
siduously to involve businessmen more deeply in these
endeavors. However, these efforts met with only limited
success because business involvement, in my opinion,
will not be effectively enlisted without a real prospect
of business profit. American business is not a charitable
foundation nor a social service agency. It functions to
make a fair return to its principals or its shareholders.
It cannot do otherwise without weakening the economic
strength of the country, which is the only sure basis for
remedying its ills. Perhaps the new administration can
elicit a better response. Perhaps the tax credit would
intensify the involvement of business and industry in
finding solutions to our social ills. More likely, there
may have to be a more radical remedy in the form of
public investment in social stability and urban tran-
quility such as we have made during the last decade for
national security and space conquest.

Somewhat akin to our quest for a cure for human
cancer, we await a breakthrough that we are hopeful
will come if enough thought, enough research, enough
energy and finally enough of our material resources of
skill and money are poured into the effort. We are all
concerned. As Governor Nelson Rockefeller recently
pointed out: "The plainest law of modern life is that so
long as there remains despair in the slums there will be
disorder in the cities." He added that if we are to save
and rebuild our cities we must be prepared to invest

$150 billion in public and private capital over the next 10 years to do the job. In other words, the problem that will make or break the future of this country is the problem of the cities.

In my view, the foremost urban problem is the plight of the slum-dwellers—the "hard-core unemployed," so-called. They must be motivated to seek jobs. They must be trained to handle them. And they must be maintained on the job. *But, first of all, the national will of the American people to meet and solve the problem of hard-core unemployment must be aroused.* I am confident that if we can make the problem visible the public will react favorably as it has always done in time of crisis. There has been a great deal of publicity about the problem and some television coverage of various dramatic projects, but the truth is that there has been only a very small amount of real work done.

We have treated the problem largely as a Public Relations effort. Brave statistics have been disseminated publicly, but behind this facade of figures there has been little coming to grips with the actual problem of hiring and training these people, and developing creative programs and managing them imaginatively. One program, which I find attractive, is "Project 100,000," which former Secretary of Defense McNamara instituted while in the Pentagon. Its objective is to train the previously "untrainables," to take into the Armed Services annually 100,000 young men from among those who would have otherwise been rejected because of educational deficiencies. The project grew out of the appalling draft-rejection rate which McNamara discovered. In 1966, he points out in his book, *The Essence of Security*, out of 1.8 million young men reaching military service age in the United States, almost 600,000—fully a third—failed to qualify. In some states the rejection rate ran to 60 percent and for some states among Negroes it exceeded 80 percent. McNamara reasoned: "If so massive a number of our young men were educationally unqualified for even the least complicated tasks of military service, how could they reasonably be expected to lead productive and rewarding lives in an increasingly technological and highly skilled society?"

Department of Defense studies showed that a great number of those rejected were the hapless and hopeless victims of poverty. At McNamara's urging the Department began to give these men the benefit of its experience in educational innovation and on-the-job training in an atmosphere of high motivation and morale. The idea was to return them, after their tour of duty, to civilian life equipped with new skills and attitudes with which they could break out of the self-perpetuating poverty cycle. After the first year, during which 49,000 were taken into the "Project 100,000" program, 98 percent successfully graduated from basic training. These men were then sent out among various service units but never singled out or stigmatized as a special group. For the purposes of internal record-keeping within the Department they were termed "New Standards Men," but the men themselves were never told they were in a special category.

Final results can only be evaluated after the men complete their two-year tour of duty and are returned to civilian life. However, Mr. McNamara insists that "the plain fact is that Project 100,000 is succeeding even beyond the most hopeful expectations." The former Defense Secretary said recently that he is convinced that the "Project 100,000" men will continue to do a creditable job in the services and that on return to civilian life their earning capacity and their overall achievement in society will be two or three times what they would have been without the program.

These are hopeful signs and should properly be pitted in the public mind against the wave of insistent demands we have been getting for more stringent police action to put down disturbances that result from hopelessness within the inner city. Police action is definitely not the answer. Such action will not provide a solution. We have to get to the root of the problem with imaginative and creative ideas and programs. What we need is fewer slogans and more solutions. We have got to get at such things as much better and much more uniform police training—training that will result in crime prevention instead of more criminal arrests. Some of our big cities, such as New York and Los Angeles, have recently increased their efforts in this field. Demands for a better-paid police force must also generate better-trained police forces, not solely in the matter of containing riots but in the more fundamental area of preventing them. There have been suggestions of establishing a National Police Academy, comparable to the military service academies, at which selected members of police departments throughout the country would be versed in the cultural background and economic history of the ghettoes as well as in marksmanship. The objective would be to make them more fully informed of the nature and psychology of the neighborhoods in which they operate and consequently better prepared to maintain order rather than merely restore it when disrupted. These are worthy objectives and perhaps they should be sought in parallel with the more immediate efforts of providing meaningful jobs for the hard-core. There is a definite relationship between crime and employment as I will show in later statistics.

We also have a broad educational challenge, far beyond the challenge of education and training our poor and our unemployed for jobs: We must make the entire country aware of the anomaly of unprecedented prosperity on the one hand and the pockets of misery and and privation and despair that represent 10 percent of our people. We must especially take note of the fact that as prosperity has risen, the lot of the hard-core unemployed and the ghetto dweller has worsened relatively.

It is impossible for the bulk of our people to believe that with all our prosperity, we still have a real problem in poverty. Those with jobs sometimes scornfully adorn their new-car bumpers with stickers that say, "I'm Fighting Poverty—I'm Working." Others point to the teeming want-ad sections of our metropolitan newspapers and ask, "There are jobs aplenty—why don't these people get to work?"

Although they do not mean to be callous, these critics do not realize what it is to want to work, but not to be able to get a job because of lack of education, or skill, or experience—or all three. They have never known the handicap of the man who is jobless through no fault of his own, but because there is no longer any demand for the unskilled laborer. They have never known the frustrations of the ghetto resident. They have never known the handicap of color.

One of the marvels of American civilization—one of the achievements of American life in which we can all take pride—is the glory of the hundreds and even thousands of poor-born Americans who have risen by guts and sweat, training and opportunity from the lower depths of the inner city to positions of responsibility and leadership. They are in business and the professions, they are in public life and social service, they are among our scientists and explorers. However it would be too much to expect all of them to surmount without additional help the disadvantages and hobbling conditions of the ghetto. As a people, we have many heroes who were in positions of leadership in the conquest of this continent. We shall never know the immensity of their effort or suffer the trial of those who fell by the wayside in this historic march to our present greatness. Nor shall we ever know how many more heroes we could have had if only some proper opportunity had been offered some now unsung genius at a critical juncture in his life. This applies particularly to the Black American throughout the country, the Mexican American in the Southwest, the Puerto Ricans on the East Coast, and the American Indian.

All we can do now and what we must do now is to make the problem visible. We have got to define the problem of poverty, which also comprises race relations, to our fellow Americans so that it will be credible to all those whose heads are now in the sand.

Recently, while in Vienna, I toured the poorest sections of the city. There, it seems to me, the lot of the poor was not as hopeless as it seems to be in America. The poor in Vienna—and presumably other cities in Europe—somehow keep busy and somehow manage to maintain their self-respect. They are not up against the racial complexities of our society. We must also realize that in some respects, the ghetto problem in certain European countries was solved by police action. But that is an idea we cannot entertain because it is wholly repugnant to our traditions of freedom and opportunity.

What, then, can we do? Let me give you some answers based on (1) my experience with the President's Test Program for Job Development to ease the hard-core unemployment problem in five test cities, (2) the experience of my company, Aerojet-General Corporation, in setting up a self-supporting, profit-oriented subsidiary in the heart of the Watts area of Los Angeles, and (3) the prospective use of space-technology techniques in solving other urban problems.

First of all let me say that I retain two lasting impressions from my work with the five-city Test Program in which I was engaged in Washington from October 1967 through January of this year. First, we are in deep trouble as a nation if we cannot soon evaluate the nature and extent of our urban problems, particularly with respect to the hard-core unemployed, both the young and the not-so-young. Second, the business and industrial community—in other words, private enterprise—must take the leadership and assume a major hand in the solution of these problems. We must do this as a matter of economic necessity, if for no other reason. Unless we take prompt, effective and nation-wide action the eventual cost may be much greater—in terms of dollars, in terms of wasted lives and in terms of civil turmoil.

I do not want to overemphasize the bleakness of the outlook. I would prefer to stress that during the brief period of the Test Program I found exhilarating the fine response that came from the private sector in the five cities we visited. There was real readiness to provide imaginative programs for meaningful jobs. Many different approaches were suggested and a whole spectrum of opportunities offered, although many proposals did not fit the established government pattern and fell outside regular governmental practice. There were several exceptional proposals that required policy decisions at the highest level. Regrettably in such cases, inevitable but none the less intolerable delays in government action frustrated the proposals. As of January 1 of this year, more than 100 proposals had been submitted. The most significant and, in my opinion, those providing the best opportunity for lasting solution of the problem *were not the typical on-the-job training type.*

Eventually, contracts were issued covering 6414 trainees at a total cost of $13,000,000. Costs varied from $775 to nearly $5000 per trainee, with the average at about the $2000 level. I would like to emphasize that the average cost of $2000 is of less interest to me than the nature of the better programs. The higher-cost ones were clearly a better investment because they gave promise of transforming the trainee into a responsible, full-time worker and taxpayer. One program, which will cost about $10,000 per trainee, is to me among the most imaginative of the lot—and happily has recently been authorized by the Department of Labor. The unusual program to which I refer was proposed by the largest repair service organization in our country. They are engaging 400 of the hard-core in a cumulative, progressive program under which the more able will graduate to more difficult and demanding jobs, and eventually the more enterprising will be assisted in going into business for themselves and thus be in a position to hire others within their communities. The first step will be to teach the trainee to handle comparatively simple operations—the repair of small appliances such as toasters, electric irons, vacuum cleaners—and to guarantee a job to those who complete the training. Those with a capability to go further will then be trained to repair larger and more complicated appliances, refrigerators, washing machines and the like. Those who can go still further will be taught radio repair work, with each level, of course, giving higher earnings. The more competent of the radio repairmen will in turn be trained to handle television repairs. Eventually, those reaching the highest level will be instructed in keeping books of accounts, so they could set up their own shops within the ghetto itself and employ others. The company further has agreed to stick with the trainees on a "Big Brother" basis for two years, help them set up an inventory, obtain small-business loans and otherwise give them a maximum opportunity to succeed. By this means, persons who had been a burden to the community will become regular employees *or even employers* and move into the taxpaying group of the economy. My arithmetic says that in a very short time we will have our investment back. According to the company that undertook this program, the American economy needs an additional 25,000 TV repairmen annually. It is also important to consider that these trainees will provide services largely in the ghetto areas where even the poorest homes have radio and television sets and where it has been difficult to obtain service in the past.

Such programs reflect the readiness I found for business to undertake in flexible fashion a number of different efforts. These programs should be closely monitored to determine which ones are the most effective. At the same time, we should realize that the solutions we seek are as multi-faceted as the problem itself, and it is going to take time to iron out the difficulties. Many of you may be familiar with the AVCO, Raytheon, Fairmicco, Lockheed, LTV, Thiokol and other programs that have received a fair amount of publicity, so I will not go into them. But they are all noble experiments of the type I wish to succeed. Many of them stem from the Test Program. I think their success should encourage other businessmen to "get their feet wet" by establishing plants or hiring the "unemployables" of our ghettos. That is, what is urgently needed, I think, is some overall organizational leadership to stimulate additional programs. The Test Programs covered only five cities—Boston, Washington, Chicago, San Antonio and Los Angeles. Its results were positive and now call for a much broader application of this concept throughout the country. To begin with we need an equivalent of a National Security Council to assure all federal resources are marshalled and coordinated toward measuring and solving the urban problem. Also, a unified command is needed with the authority of the White House to direct the use of all funds authorized by Congress for the purpose of alleviating the urban problem. This unified command should serve as a single point of contact for the private sector as well as for the state and local governments. We licked the unemployment problem in the Thirties, when 25 percent of our work force was jobless. Certainly we can find the means and the will to sharply reduce the smaller percentage which still plagues our inner cities. We cannot lick it if we concern ourselves with only a few thousand of the millions still unemployed. We cannot lick it if we do not coordinate the employment problem with those of housing, social welfare, pollution, transportation, and a host of other ills that poison the atmosphere of the inner city and warp the attitudes of its inhabitants. We cannot lick it with the nightsticks of the policemen or the bayonets of the National Guard or regular troops. We can lick it only when we have carefully measured its dimensions, probed into its multiple causes and devised sophisticated means of meeting it with the best technology we can apply under the leadership of the private enterprise that made this country the most productive and the most progressive that the world has ever known.

Joblessness is not part of the personal experience of most Americans today. Much of it is invisible to the average citizen who rushes to his work by commuter train or over the freeways. Reliable statistics are hard to

come by. Somehow, the American people must be made
to feel the size and portent of the problem. The national
will must be stimulated to demand action. The most immediate need is for hard facts on who are the hard-core
unemployed and underemployed. How many are there?
Where are they? Are there 500,000 or three times that
number? In the Test Program, we found estimates in the
communities we visited varied by 300 to 500 percent. I
think the government should immediately undertake a
thorough evaluation of the situation. The data collected
should be distributed throughout the government and
the business community. Techniques should be developed that would insure continued feedback and updat-
ing. Above all, we must maintain a flexible approach. I
think it is a serious mistake to decide upon one specific
manner of getting jobs for the hard-core unemployed.
Emphasis should be given to a broad spectrum of approaches where the businessman writes his own ticket,
with the government offsetting extra costs and also providing for a reasonable profit opportunity.

Let me now say a few words about our Watts Plant
in Los Angeles because it was one of the pioneering
efforts in the field of training and giving meaningful employment to ghetto residents. It came about this way.
Soon after the 1965 riots in Los Angeles subsided, it
became obvious that jobs had to be created for residents
of the area if we were not to have an even more destructive repeat performance. We began talking with Negro
leaders in Watts and with governmental leaders as well
to see how Aerojet could help. As a result the Watts
Manufacturing Company was incorporated in August,

1966 as a subsidiary of Aerojet-General. The president of the Company is a Negro business leader, Jim Woods, who resides in the area and is well aware of its problems. When the Company was started we did not have any business, but we were certain that we could do more for Watts by putting in a plant there than by trying to absorb 500 Watts residents into our regular work force at plants which were 20 and 30 miles away, in a city which has inadequate public transportation. After considerable effort, we obtained a contract for the construction of large hospital tents for the military services. We invested a total of $1.3 million in the project and more recently we have expanded our product lines to woodworking and metalwork. The labor force of close to 500 was recruited almost entirely from the Watts area. Without advertising for help, we had 5000 applications for the several hundred jobs originally available. This convinced us the desire to work exists among the hard-core unemployed. We hired these people without restrictions. We did not care if they had police records or whether they had ever held a job before. All we expected was willingness to work and ability to respond to minimum training. We had problems. Initially, absenteeism was high. The turnover was about 6 percent per month, double the national average. But today, Watts Manufacturing Company is a growing concern. Our problem is not finding workers, but providing an adequate workload to sustain the work force.

Besides the plant in Watts, we have established two plants in Arkansas, in areas of previously high unemployment—Batesville and Camden. We employ about

1000 persons in each of these plants. We feel it is important to establish facilities in rural areas because this helps
prevent migration of the rural unemployed to already
overcrowded urban areas.

Our company's experience leads me to conclude
that in order to establish meaningful business and industry in rural or urban poverty areas, private enterprise
must go a bit beyond conventional methods of doing
business. Companies, in some instances, may have to
operate outside their major field of interest as Aerojet
and AVCO (both essentially aerospace companies) have,
going into tent-making and training printers. Flexibility,
I think, is the name of the game we must play to be
really successful in the inner city today.

We have made a beginning, but only a small beginning.

Let me now turn to the correlation between the
urban problems I have been discussing and others such
as pollution, transportation, crime control, and communications and the applicability of space-age research to
their solution. Within the past decade and a half, in order
to meet the needs of the space age, in order to bolster our
defenses with rocket-launched weapons and to expand
our knowledge of the universe through space explora-
tion, the historic rivalry between government and private
industry had to be abated. Previously highly competitive
private firms virtually merged their talents and knowledge to meet the difficult, complicated and costly needs
of the hour. We could not have accomplished the job
otherwise. Together—with the government providing the
funds and the industrial firms working harmoniously to-

gether under independent overall managerial direction—
we sent teams of men into space and hopefully will soon
send them to the moon. If we can do this for the military
security and international prestige of the United States,
we can do as much—given the will—for the internal security of the state and the solution of the urban problems that tend to divide us as a people into the America
we see on television and the "other America" which is
almost unseen in the ghettoes.

Secretary of Defense Clark Clifford recently told a
businessmen's group in Washington that "there is a real
potential for defense industry to bring enterprise to the
ghetto." He pointed to what he called "the already encouraging examples" of Watts in Los Angeles and the
Roxbury project in Boston and noted that more than 50
major defense contractors have launched specific projects.
One of these is the Lockheed project in the San Antonio
area, where there is a large Mexican-American population.

The Secretary of Defense is taking steps to encourage major contractors to give greater attention to the
possibility of locating new facilities in or near labor-
surplus areas. Through these efforts he wants to spotlight
the responsibility shared by the Defense Department in
contributing, wherever possible, to solving the problems
of hard-core unemployment. This step is significant for
two reasons: The Defense Department is responsible for
the expenditure of tens of billions of dollars a year. The
shift in emphasis represents a new philosophy that national strength and security is broader than military man-
power and ordnance. As Secretary Clifford said:

We now have a military-industrial team with unique resources of experience, engineering talent, management and problem-solving capacities, a team that must be used to help find the answers to complex weapons systems. Those answers can be put to good use by our cities and our states, by our schools, by large and small business alike. The nation will be the better and the stronger.

This is a proper place, I believe, to review briefly four important socio-economic projects that were carried on by aerospace companies in California. These are projects which drew national attention and which have since been studied by officials of various states and of some of our largest cities. In these projects, we tried to apply the systems approach to the solution of major problems common to our states and cities today.

California's problems are not those of a sparsely settled area, but of a highly industrialized state plagued by waste and pollution, crime and delinquency, chaotic transportation, and costly information procedures. These were the four categories attacked in studies made by four aerospace companies at the request of the state government. All four problems were critical to the future of the state. They were sufficiently different to test the application of systems analysis under various conditions. They involved a large number of state agencies. And they were of sufficient interest and concern as to warrant the eventual expenditure of considerable sums of money to implement programs if sound and feasible plans emerged from the studies.

I cite the four problems because I firmly believe that the managerial techniques developed to meet the requirements of the space age can be applied practically to the changing urban environment and the solution of our urban problems if means can be found to finance such efforts properly. This must be done either on a regional basis or by the federal government responding to a strong expression of the national will that our urban problems be solved, not by police power, but through modern, scientific means now at our disposal through profit-oriented private enterprise.

These were the four programs:

THE WASTE DISPOSAL STUDY

The waste disposal study was intended to develop broad guidelines for the establishment of a complete system to manage waste disposal. This involved the transportation, treatment, and removal of waste materials to prevent and minimize pollution of the land, air, and water of the state. The researchers assembled data obtained from many industrial, agricultural, recreational, and medical sources as well as state and local government agencies. Importantly, the study pointed out that to be effective waste management must be applied within a system covering all wastes. It suggested that a single agency be held responsible for the overall problem and recommended a program to define objectives.

In this study, as in the others, I would like to note, the emphasis is on the systems approach to a solution. The problem of all wastes had to be considered. For instance, it would not have done to package up tons of air pollutants and then get rid of them where they would pollute streams or the ocean; nor would it be practical to burn or otherwise chemically destroy solid wastes and thereby add to the air pollution.

Similarly, in dealing with crime detection and delinquency, the factors of housing, income, population density, education, and other factors had to be coordinated with employment statistics. I will discuss this study in more detail now, for I think it is crucial to the urban environment, which is my topic today. It is also indicative of the role business must be called upon to play in solving the problems of the inner city.

THE CRIME PREVENTION AND DELINQUENCY PROGRAM

The study of crime prevention and delinquency was intended to develop new practices to handle these problems, which would save the state millions of dollars now spent in correctional measures and institutions and prevent other millions lost through the depredations of the criminal and delinquent on thousands of individuals throughout the state. Ironically, this crime prevention study was completed just before the Watts riots of 1965. It accurately pinpointed the source of maximum danger to the Los Angeles community. Five separate overlays were made to cover a map of Los Angeles county, noting:

1. Areas where median family income was less than $5000.

2. Areas where Negroes comprised 75 percent or more of the population.

3. Maximum population density areas (10,000 or more per square mile).
4. Maximum school drop-out areas.
5. Maximum crime-rate areas.

These overlays all met over the Watts area of Los Angeles, giving a clear indication of the trouble area which broke into deadly conflagration a few weeks later. I mention these details to emphasize the accuracy with which space-age methods can analyze local situations.

The analysis of statistics on California's crime and delinquency problems gave a strong indication of the fact that the extremely rapid rise in the crime rate might not be solely due to the fact that society is displaying significantly more criminal tendencies, but rather because the population in the age group which contributes most to crime is rapidly increasing. In order to understand this phenomenon more clearly it is necessary to realize that the major portion of the offenders are between 14 and 29 years of age.

Although the crime rates are relatively constant, adult rates were shown to be decreasing slightly while juvenile rates were rising slightly (at a maximum of 3.27 percent a year). Based on these results and extrapolating into the future, the study indicated we can expect to have a level of criminal activity in the next five years which will be 30 percent greater than it is this year, with an increase from 1960 to 1975 of greater than 100 percent. This assumes the relative constancy in the crime rate experienced in California over the past few years. If external conditions change for the worse, unemployment increases, or other factors change significantly during these next few years, then the seriousness of the problem will increase. From 1960 to 1975 the age group from which most criminal offenders come (14 to 29 years) in California is expected to increase 110 percent, almost twice the expected 60 percent increase of the total population. Crime is indeed increasing faster than population, but primarily as a result of the increase in the number of members of the age group responsible for most of the crime. This age group that causes the most crimes, as you might expect, is composed largely of the "war babies" of the World War II era and the children born in the postwar era. Whether there will be a downturn in the proportion of this age group after 1975, when the effects of birth-control practices and of "The Pill" may be felt, was not statistically evaluated.

If we are to deal properly, from the standpoint of crime prevention, with the group that contributes most heavily to crime and the high cost of crime to the community, we must learn much more about the group than we now know.

The principal investigator in the Crime and Delinquency Study I cite, when asked to what extent he believes stronger police action will reduce crime, stated "In the overall picture, it will have no measurable effect." He added that he was convinced that employment—meaningful jobs—was the only effective and practical solution to reducing significantly the level of criminal activity, particularly in the critical age group 14 to 29.

Despite much sloganeering about "crime does not pay" and the efforts of "Big Brothers" and other volunteer groups with good intentions but little hard information or expertise in the field, crime-prevention programs have for the most part been neglected in the past. However, great potential benefits could be derived from such programs because they are directly related to other programs designed to fight poverty and to provide opportunity for the youth of this country. Once this relationship is truly appreciated, real efforts should be made at crime prevention on a scientific basis. I feel that we would not only save millions of dollars now lost to crime through theft, arson, riots, mounting costs of protection, including police, private guards, insurance, and so on, but that also a positive gain in profits and services as well as in the taxable income of the newly employed would be made.

Crime prevention programs must keep individuals from entering into and cycling through the system of criminal justice. If we could achieve such prevention in even only moderate measure to begin with, we could save the expenditure of millions of dollars for court action, correctional institutions, rehabilitation centers, and other appurtenances of the judicial and penal processes. However, today, most systems of government expend only a relatively small amount of effort to prevent crime and delinquency taken in the broadest sense of the terms. I believe deeply that science can aid effectively in the development of concepts and in the conduct of research into new approaches to the prevention of crime and delinquency.

The study we made disclosed that certain socioeconomic factors, when combined in the environment of a group, produce a condition which causes the group to be highly susceptible to criminal activity. A corollary concept indicates that population density of the group also serves to aggravate its delinquency susceptibility. Thus, in the area that eventually became involved in destructive riots, unemployment averaged twice that of Los Angeles county as a whole, and approximately 35 percent of the families in the area earned less than $4000 a year. Also the population density was approximately three times that of the Los Angeles basin.

Further, education is of key importance to job-holding and adjustment in modern society. It is very important that all youths, especially those in the susceptible group, be assisted in obtaining a meaningful education, personal orientation, and in the development of vocational and functional skills. A Youth Assistance Program is needed to provide academic, social, and psychological development for a significantly large number of potential offenders. This conclusion comes easily when we note that 45 percent of the 6.7 million youths in the United States between the ages of 16 and 21 dropped out before completing high school and that the unemployment rates for the drop-outs is 27 percent—twice as high as for high school graduates. However, fully 70 percent of the drop-outs are well within the range of average intellect and could have been made useful and productive citizens if they had been reached in time to bring them into the mainstream of our industrial society.

I will touch only briefly on the other two study programs carried on for California by aerospace companies. Dealing with state-wide correlation of information and with transportation, they are of significance to large cities and have direct bearing on the urban environment.

The State-wide information study was intended to provide a coordinated approach to data gathering, processing, storage, and retrieval that would achieve substantial cost savings over present methods and give interested agencies greater accessibility to the information. *The transportation study* involved the design of an integrated land, sea, and air transportation network within the state and the specification of a program to solve the problem.

The question posed by California in these four study contracts was whether technology, through the systems-analysis approach, could shed light on some of the problems that face a modern community. The aerospace companies involved in the programs, Aerojet-General, Space-General, Lockheed and North American, were not asked to formulate new goals for the state, nor to make policy decisions. What was hoped for *and what was accomplished* was the formulation in clear unambiguous terms of the decisions that would have to be made. The implementation of these decisions is now in the hands of the state government authorities. Unfortunately, like everything or nearly everything else in life that is worthwhile, the price is high. Financial means must be found eventually to implement the programs developed for the state.

These pioneer studies inspired similar efforts by some of our larger cities and discussion in Congress, which revolved on the possibility of seeking solutions to regional problems, involving groups of states, by a similar systems-analysis approach. Those of us in management who know the value of such an approach look forward to the day when a higher priority will be given these programs and when we can demonstrate in practice the effectiveness of the solutions developed by technology. We are hopeful, but we also realize that a heavy commitment of funds is essential to such programs, as they have been to the space program. The major problem, as I have indicated earlier, is to find some profit-oriented mechanism by which the great talents of the systems-oriented industry can be brought to bear on the needs of our cities and states.

Since the beginning of World War II, the urban environment has changed radically. Mobility has been one of the hallmarks of this change. Although there are few statistics on the subject, we are all well aware of the vast displacements that took place throughout the nation between the early 1930's and the late 1960's. The old sense of neighborliness and neighborhood based upon reasonable permanence of location gave way to temporary residence and resentment toward rather than understanding of near-residents who came from strange places, sometimes spoke with a strange accent and often had strange ideas. The turnover was phenomenal as thousands upon thousands came and went as job requirements, the local economy, or personal preference dictated. Not only was the sense of community entirely lost by the migrants, but the loss rubbed off as well on the older and more permanent residents of an area who themselves moved into the newly developing suburbs. Thus the inner city disintegrated because it came to be a combination of temporary and disharmonious parts. The tolerance that had long existed in city areas inhabited by Poles, Germans, Italians, Jews, and other ethnic groups

broke down under the impact of Negro and white migrants, Puerto Ricans, and the exiled Europeans who
came to America to escape Hitler, Mussolini, Stalin, and
other dictatorships in the Old World. Strange languages
were heard and strange customs appeared in the old,
accustomed, erstwhile comfortable quarters of our cities.
Intolerance, which has been described as dislike of the
unlike, took root in areas where somnolent acquiescence
of neighbors' idiosyncracies had formerly prevailed.

The unquestioned appeal of urban life to the rural
dispossessed in the last 20 or 30 years has brought an
influx into our more populous centers that is reminiscent
of the late nineteenth-century and early twentieth-cen-
tury movement to our shores from Europe. Cities such as
New York, Chicago, Los Angeles, Detroit, Cleveland, and
many others have been the particular targets of Negro
migrants from the South and Southwest. At the same
time rural whites from our central states have migrated
in large numbers to industrial centers on both coasts and
in the Great Lakes region.

Combined with this factor of migration has been the
sensational increase in the mechanization of industry and
the startling technological advances in production, management, and other aspects of industrial progress. These
have tended to enlarge and even exaggerate the already
existing differences between the simple and pragmatic
life of the rural poor and the competitive, sophisticated
socio-economic life of the new city and its suburbs. The
proliferation of communications media, particularly of
radio and television, has multiplied the frustrations of the
dispossessed in the face of the glamorous affluence por-

trayed surrounding them. In new surroundings where only jobs and money can buy necessities and enliven the promise of a better life, most of the migrants found themselves relegated to the disintegrating sections of the cities, living on the edge of poverty or supported by relief, with little interest in and little ability to take advantage of educational and training opportunities that could fit them to become productive factors in their new environment, as they had been, to some extent at least, in the old.

Business did not create these problems, but business, as the most creative agent in American life today, must be counted on to offer practical solutions to them. I think we can accept it as an axiom in American life that when business (or industry) is offered a profitable venture, it manages to find solutions to our social problems. For example, the toll roads, which opened up the wilderness of young America, and the canal routes and the railroads, all were subsidized by the government but developed and managed by private enterprise. Our vast air traffic today, as well as our overland highway transport, depends upon government support, as do such socially effective institutions as Social Security, insured bank accounts, Medicare, and help for dependents of all ages in our population. The vast expansion undertaken in the housing field has been equally dependent upon government support for its initiative and financing.

My experience in Washington with the Test Program and my company's experience in Watts lead me to conclude that, in order to establish meaningful business and industrial programs to take care of the hard-core unemployed, companies must be prepared to go a bit beyond their conventional methods of doing business. So must governments—not only with respect to the unemployed, but with respect to the total environment of the community, urban or rural. Again I would emphasize flexibility is required to be really successful in meeting our urban problems.

Regrettably, many problems still remain largely undefined and our people become aware of them only when they manifest themselves in riots, burnings, marches, civil disorder, and unnatural racial tensions. The misery of the situation is mostly invisible to and unfelt by the majority of our citizens. *I feel strongly that somehow the national will for urgent action must be aroused.* Once this is done, I am confident that government and business will dovetail their capabilities, their powers and their resources toward finding solid, meaningful, and, hopefully, lasting solutions.

The urban environment is not an inconquerable frontier. Sooner or later it will give way, as all our frontiers have in the past, to the march of progress, which industry leads when the profit criterion of our traditional free enterprise system beckons.

I trust that in some measure the Moskowitz lectures and other symposia which New York University has sponsored, as well as somewhat similar projects elsewhere, will stimulate national interest in our urban problems and ultimately promote the national will to hitch our capabilities to our vision in their solution.

JOBS: A KEY TO IMPROVING THE URBAN ENVIRONMENT

by Paul H. Douglas

G. K. CHESTERTON once remarked that the most important event that happened in England towards the end of eighteenth century was an event that happened in France, namely, the French Revolution. It can similarly be said that the most important event which has happened in American cities during these last tumultous decades has been an event which has happened on the farms, namely, the agricultural revolution. It is this fact which has helped to change the nature of our urban population and to alter the educational and other problems which the modern metropolis must face.

I repeat that the central force which has quietly operated below the surface of American life during the last quarter of a century has been the unprecedented migration of people from the farms to the metropolitan centers. In 1940, according to the census, there were 30.5 million people living on the farms, or 23 percent of the total population of 132.6 million. In 1966, however, there were only 11.6 million, or 5.9 percent of the total population of 194 million. Today the total numbers are not more than 11 million out of a total of 200 million, or about 5.5 percent. Probably the actual figure is a little less.

I

There has, therefore, been a net migration in a little over a quarter of a century of no less than 19 million people previously attached to the soil and a decline in their relative proportions of the American population to only one-fourth of what they were only 28 short years ago. During this time, the number of farms has decreased from 6⅓ million to less than half this figure, while the average size of a farm has approximately doubled. The small farmers, the tenants and laborers are the ones who have pulled up stakes and left the soil in such unprecedented numbers.

This shift in population from the farms to the metropolitan areas has been particularly marked among the younger folks. They have felt fewer ties to the soil and they have been less afraid of facing the unfamiliar problems of the cities. I well remember being told, some years ago, by a ruddy-faced Illinois farmer that he, at the age of 45, was the youngest farmer in his prosperous rural county. I also recall how when I was canvassing for votes in one of my campaigns, I went into the hometown of Burl Ives, the way-faring folk singer, which, according to his autobiography, had been in his youth a gay and adventurous village, and finding that house after house was either empty or lived in by an ancient couple who shuffled uncertainly to the door.

This transfer of population is unprecedented in the history of our country. It has been far greater in volume than that caused by the British Enclosures Acts which have been so graphically chronicled by the Hammonds. It was not effected, like the shift in population in England was, by legal compulsion, but rather by the operation of economic forces which have at once squeezed workers off the soil and attracted them to the urban areas.

The propulsive forces have, of course, been the development of farm machinery such as the tractor, the cotton picker, and the multiple plows that have enabled a man to cultivate far more acres than he could before, together with the various other improvements in hybrid seed, more and better fertilizer, and other methods of cultivation which have increased productivity per man in agriculture by appreciably more than in manufacturing. Thus, between 1947 and 1967 the productivity of the farmers increased by nearly two-and-a-half times to a relative index of 344, while that for all nonfarm occupations rose by only 72 percent to an index of 172, and that for manufacturing occupations to 178.[1] At the same time, the inelastic nature of the demand for farm products, whether measured in terms of prices or income, has kept down the price of farm products in relation to the general price level, for as real incomes have increased, the wants of people have expanded into other fields than food.

1 *Handbook of Labor Statistics*, 1968, p. 122.

City life, moreover, with its higher average money incomes, has always exercised a strong attraction for rural folks.

A further idea of the extent of this migration can be gained from the fact that there were 29.8 million people, or over 18 percent of the population in 1960, who were living in a different county than they had lived in five years before. Six years later, in 1966, there were no less than 12.5 million people, or 6.6 percent of the population, living in a different county than they had lived in during the preceding year. This in itself shows a speeding up in the rate of migration—namely, as much movement was carried out in three years as previously required five. Half of this number, moreover, or 3.3 percent of the total, were living in a different state than they were during the preceding year.[2]

All this by now either is or should be well known. What for some years was less appreciated were the problems of adjustment which the migrants faced. They were not only the untrained young but the less skilled adults. They were not trained for the trades and occupations of the cities and towns. Although the successful farmer needs a great deal of varied skills, those who went to the cities did not have even these, for they were the poorer and least successful farmers and farm laborers. They were hand, not machine, workers. The tractor, the planter and the cotton picker had made their hand labor largely obsolete. Many of these migrants caught on in the cities and towns into which they moved and found both jobs and a higher material standard of living, but large num-

2 *Statistical Abstract of the U.S.*, pp, 34–35.

bers did not. It is they who have largely manifested the peculiar problems which today afflict our cities. Just as it was the flood of immigrants from Northern and Western Europe which differentiated our urban growth from that of Europe during the half century from 1840 to 1890, and from Southern and Eastern Europe during the quarter century from 1890 to 1914, so in the last quarter of a century it has been the migration from our own farms which has colored and complicated our urban life. A large part of these have been Negroes who in a quarter of a century have been transformed from a rural to an urban people.

Millions accustomed to living in rural poverty are now forced to live in urban poverty and find it more impersonal, more frightening, and more degrading than that which they experienced as dwellers in the land of cotton, as Appalachians, or as hard-scrabble farmers. I shall confine myself primarly to only one of the problems which they and other youngsters face; namely, that of getting jobs and establishing an economic foothold in an alien world.

In addition, the high birth rates of the period from 1945 to 1950 have, of course, brought into the labor market an added group of young workers. In 1945 the surplus of births over deaths amounted to 1.4 million, while in 1950 this came to 2.2 million. These children are now coming into maturity.

The combination of the coming of age of the boys and girls born in this period of high net fertility and of internal migration has enormously increased the number of persons, and particularly of young people, who must find work in urban areas. This has resulted in a high rate of unemployment for the urban young. Dr. James R. Conant was acute enough to notice this a decade ago and prophetically referred to it as "social dynamite." Although the official rate of unemployment has gone down from the 7 percent of 1960 to half this rate at present it is still unconscionably high, especially for young people of the slums and particularly for the young Negro slum dwellers. Let us look at the official rates for 1967.

PERCENTAGE OF UNEMPLOYMENT AMONG YOUNG IN 1967 [a]

Group	16–17 Years	18–19 Years	20–24 Years
Male Whites	12.7	9.0	4.2
Female Whites	12.9	10.6	6.0
Male Nonwhites	28.9	20.1	8.0
Female Nonwhites	32.0	28.3	13.8

a *Handbook of Labor Statistics,* 1968, pp. 97–99.

These statistics are bad enough for the white boys and girls of 16 and 17 years because one out of eight is shown to be out of work, whereas one out of every ten or eleven of the 18- and 19-year-olds is in a similar plight. However, for the nonwhites or Negroes, the figures are even more shocking. A third of the girls and two-sevenths of the boys in the 16-to-17-year group had no jobs at all, nor did two-sevenths of the girls and one-fifth of the boys who were 18 and 19. When the white youngsters moved into the 20-to-24-year class, most of them managed to get work, so that the unemployment rate fell to 4.2 and 6.0 percent, respectively. However, the Negroes did not do nearly so well. Their rates of unemployment, while lower than before, were still twice those of the corresponding age group among the whites, amounting to 8 percent for the young men and no less than 14 percent for the young women.

These statistics tell only a part of the story, for they cover only those "able to work, willing to work, but unable to find suitable employment." They do not cover those who for one reason or another have given up systematically seeking to find employment. Nor do they take account of the millions whom the census has never been able to count and who sleep in alleys, abandoned autos, and vacant dilapidated houses. The census has made an estimate that these uncounted, who statistically are nonpersons, amount to a total of nearly 6 million. This ratio is particularly high among Negro youth. There is little doubt that in some slum ghettos the rate of unemployment for the 16- to 17-year-olds may run as high as 40 to 50 percent and that they continue at high rates up to and indeed including full manhood.

These groups, together with the boys and girls under 16 whom they influence and those from 20 to 24 into whose ranks they graduate, are immediately responsible for most of the added disorder and crime that has broken out in our cities during the last three years.

How to deal with this tendency is indeed one of the most serious of our modern problems. While fully recognizing the need for vigorous protective action as a deterrent, I want to urge as strongly as I can that these young folks should not be treated as lost souls. As a result of a variety of causes, which are largely not their fault, they have been given a bad start and have been surrounded by almost every conceivable difficulty. Certainly with proper care and attention a large proportion can be saved for lives of usefulness. This is one of the central tasks which this nation faces. To ignore it, or to carry out blind retaliation, is to invite deep trouble. The official figures show a total of 448 thousand boys from 16 to 19 inclusive who were unemployed in 1967, and 235 thousand more males from 20 to 24 who were out of work. The corresponding number of girls from 16 to 19 who were out of work was 391 thousand with another 277,000 in the 20-to-24-year class who were unemployed. The official total for both sexes would be 837,000 for those from 16 to 19 years of age inclusive and 512,000 for those in the 20-to-24-year group. This is a combined total of 1,349,000, or about 1⅓ million. However, the real total, for the reasons which I have mentioned, was much greater than this and probably would be at least over 2 million plus the youngsters under 16 who are outside the jurisdiction of the criminal courts and are more and more being used by the older boys to commit the actual acts of violence.

The need is, therefore, huge. It cannot be disregarded.

II

I wish to propose a three-point program, which I regard as a minimum.

(1) The federal, state, and local governments should create a half million new jobs for the youth of our country. The pay for this work could be at a learner's rate of around $1.50 an hour or $60 a week. The total salary cost would be close to $1½ billion a year, with supplies and equipment amounting to another billion, for a total cost of $2½ billion. There will be complaints that we cannot afford such a sum. To me it is more important than putting a man on the moon, producing supersonic airlines, or launching the unfortunate TFX. It will certainly be even better for the community than freeing most of the oil millionaires from equitable taxation. We need a better sense of values in order to indicate to our politicians that they must do what we feel is right.

It is frequently not realized how many workers are in fact employed by the various levels of government. The census report on public employment in 1966 gives these totals, namely 2.6 million by the federal government, 2.2 million by the states, and 6.4 million by the localities, of whom 2 million were employed by the cities. This came to a combined total of 11.2 million. If we deduct the 1.2 million in state and local governments who worked less than full time, we nevertheless have the equivalent of 10 million full-time government workers. It would not seem to be an excessive requirement for all these levels of government to find useful and educative employment for 500,000 juveniles and young workers who are now unemployed, for this would only be an addition of 5 percent.

A large number of both boys and girls could be used in the local schools, where 3 million teachers are now employed. Many of these teachers are overburdened not only with pupils but also with bookkeeping and petty administrative details. Young people could take over many of these minor tasks [3] and relieve the teachers for the far more constructive work of teaching.

There were 723,000 employees in the hospitals in 1966. The hospitals are conspicuously understaffed and could employ scores of thousands of additional young women productively as nurses' assistants and in the kitchens. Boys could serve as orderlies. Over half a million workers are employed on the highways and approximately another hundred thousand in the parks and in recreation; an equal number are employed in sanitation work. The boys and young men from 16 to 24 could be employed on special projects in these fields including the extra cleaning of streets and alleys, the transformation of vacant lots into postage stamp parks, garden areas, and miniature playgrounds.

The libraries employed 45,000, and here young girls and women could help in repairing books and magazines, cataloging, and keeping records. There were 100,000 working in the financial administration and general control of the cities with many additional thousands working in public welfare, public health, housing and urban renewal, at the airports, and in the water services of the cities.

During the Depression, we developed the Works Progress Administration. Although the WPA was exposed to derision from the conservative press, it not only helped

3 Such as entering grades and keeping attendance records, cleaning blackboards, helping to preserve order, supervising recreation, and work in the kitchen and dining rooms. All of this could be made educational.

to save millions of families from starvation, but it carried out a remarkable amount of public work. At a total cost of $10 billion spread over a number of years, the WPA erected some 25,000 public buildings and constructed 650,000 miles of highways, streets, and roads; 78,000 bridges and viaducts; 24,000 miles of sidewalks and paths; 7,000 parks and playgrounds as well as improving 17,000 more. It did other useful works as well. It was a good investment.

Today with the lives of from 2 to 3 million youths at stake, and with the very peace of our cities involved, do we not have an equal challenge? We can make our cities, through projects like the WPA, shining rather than repulsive communities, and in the process save much of our most precious asset, namely, our young.

Students of public finance have emphasized the need for added federal funds to meet some of the local burdens for health, welfare, housing, street services, and education. These should be provided, but cannot part of these funds be used to finance extra work performed by youngsters who would otherwise be idle? One of our unused assets is the idle time of the unemployed. Money to put these young people to work on useful projects would be one of the most productive expenditures that could be made. This can be done if the public would only realize the need for action and make a solemn commitment to act. Do we have to wait for a catastrophe to act? If such a catastrophe were to come, it would be more likely to divide and embitter the country than unite the nation. It would make remedies more rather than less difficult to achieve.

Now that the election is over, is it too much to hope

that the men of good will in both major parties may unite around such a common purpose on both the local and national levels? In view of the mutual hostility which exists in our cities between the policemen and firemen on the one hand and the gangs of unemployed youth on the other, it would be wishful thinking to expect that any considerable number of the young gang members can themselves be quickly transformed into apprentices to the police and fire service. But a lateral indirect shift could be worked out whereby more stable youths who already have jobs could be recommended by boys clubs and settlements as younger and auxiliary members of the police and fire departments. Then the vacancies thus created could be filled from the ranks of the unemployed.

We should not neglect the possibilities offered by the housing program. President Johnson called for the construction of from 2.5 to 2.6 million units a year. This is over a million more than the average number built during the last ten years or an increase of a full 70 percent. Although it is probably impossible to reach this goal because of the shortages of skilled labor, among other things, at the very least, however, we should build at the rate of from 2 to 2¼ million units. The former figure would be over half a million more than the past average and 700,000 more than in 1967, whereas the latter would be a full 50 percent greater than the ten-year average. It would be nearly a million more than were constructed in 1967. This increased volume should be specifically aimed at providing housing for the poor and near poor who need housing the most, although, of course, a large volume should also be designed for the lower-middle and middle economic classes.

Congress has gone a long way to carry out the housing program. The funds for public housing for the poor are automatically provided for in the 1968 Housing Act itself and would seem to be beyond Congressional limitation. Whereas only $25 million instead of $75 million has been specifically appropriated for fiscal 1969 for low-interest home purchase and an equal amount for subsidized loans for low-interest rental dwellings, the sums granted should be enough to get the program started during the current half year. There will be a real test of intent, however, in the final budget approved for 1969–70.

The success of this housing program is therefore largely up to the country and to the Department of Housing and Urban Development. I personally regard it as essential to any attempt to improve life in our cities and slums. Whether the country goes through with it is the real test of whether we are in fact committed to such an effort.

I shall be an optimist and assume that we not only should be so committed but that we actually are. If we carry through such a program, this will create a large volume of added employment. It has been calculated that each housing unit will on the average not only create the opportunity for more employment for the existing labor force but will also directly cause the increase in the need for labor of an additional one-third of a man-year. Assuming that this is so, an increase of 500,000 units would create about 165,000 additional jobs, and an increase of 750,000 units about 250,000 new jobs.

A large proportion of this increase should be recruited from the unemployed youths of the slums, both black and white. Furthermore, if I know the temper of the slum dwellers and minority groups, these folks will tend to insist upon this as a necessary condition for construction. Unless they can be guaranteed a "share in the action," the black leaders may well organize to prevent the housing from being built.

There will also be a greater demand for labor in the manufacture of building materials as well as for plumbing and electrical equipment. The total number employed in 1963 in those stores which concentrated in selling building materials was 321,000 distributed as the first table indicates.[4] In addition, there were 667,000

Retail Trade	Number Employed in 1963 (in thousands)
Lumber yards	188
Heating, plumbing and electrical stores	19
Paint, glass, wallpaper	29
Hardware	85
Total	321

workers employed in the manufacture of building materials as the second table indicates.[5] We thus get a total of 988,000 or virtually a million people working in the

4 *Statistical Abstract 1967*, pp. 786–89. This does not include 225,000 employed in furniture stores.
5 *Ibid.*, pp. 740–43. This does not include those employed in the manufacture of furniture and flat glass, totaling 275,000.

Industry	*Number Employed* (in thousands)
1. Saw and planning mills	215
2. Logging camps	65
3. Millwork	130
4. Miscellaneous wooden products	62
5. Structural clay products	56
6. Concrete and plastic products	125
7. Stoves and stove products	14
Total	667

manufacture and sale of building materials. We cannot, of course, expect that the numbers employed in these trades will increase in the same proportion as the increase in building because there is much slack time that an increase in demand will take up. It would seem conservative, however, to estimate that an increase in building of one-third should create an increase of not far from one-fifth in the numbers employed and that an increase in building of one-half would approximately create an employment rise of one-third. If we were to increase output to 2 million units, we could therefore expect a further indirect increase of 200,000 jobs, and if we reached the 2¼ million mark the increase should be about 330,000. When added to the increase in the construction trades themselves, the total additional jobs that would be created would come to between 365,000 and 580,000.

The increased earnings of those employed will of

course exercise a still further stimulus to employment: The workers and allied professionals will spend more, and this will furnish a stimulus for still more jobs. I shall make no effort to estimate with any definiteness what this stimulus will be, although students of Keynes and R. F. Kahn will recognize the influence. When we were dealing with these matters in the depressed areas legislation, we used to estimate that the increased purchases by each newly employed worker would create from a half to a full additional job. If this is true, we would have at a minimum an additional stimulus of from 180,000 to 300,-000 positions. It might even go up to a half-million or more. A large portion of these secondary and tertiary jobs should also go to the young. They are indeed the chief reservoir in the nation of unused labor. The presently unemployed, as well as those newly coming in to the labor market, can and should be used to meet the added needs.

To channel a large proportion of the added jobs in construction to the poor and the presently unemployed will of course require the wholehearted cooperation of the craft unions in the building trades. I believe that under proper safeguards this will be forthcoming from most of the leading national officials. Men of the stamp of George Meany, Peter Schoeneman, Joseph Keenan, John Lyons, and Cornelius Haggerty understand what is at stake and have adopted a constructive attitude in trying to absorb the minority groups. But this cannot be said for all the local unions. I suggest that the new administration should make a try.

I personally believe that project agreements should

be negotiated for all public and publicly assisted housing. Such agreements have been entered into for work on the TVA and at the space and atomic energy installations. They provide for labor peace and for the settling of labor disputes. In this case, they could also provide for the hiring of youth and of minorities, together with plans for their training. There will just not be enough time to permit a leisurely apprentice system to be the sole means of entrance to a trade. Despite union opposition to the helper system, namely, to work beside the skilled craftsmen and to learn by doing, this seems to be the best method of breaking in the new workers. They will not be made into skilled craftsmen by this method, but they can do productive work and in return be paid a learner's rather than a craftsman's wage.

I am also one who believes that a great deal of construction work can be transferred from the site to the factory. This will carry with it the substitution of factory for handicraft labor, which will carry a lower wage rate. If factory labor is used to produce prefabricated components for the large-scale projects, it can also obtain the advantages of a more minute division of labor, a greater use of capital per worker with a resultant increase in productivity per man hour, fewer interruptions because of the weather, much lower interim financing costs, and less loss from vandalism. These lower construction costs will have a multiplied effect in the form of a lower base upon which percentages for builders' profits, architects' fees, closing costs, and write-ups for the deduction of "points" are computed. The total interest costs will also be reduced.

For these economies to be effective, however, acceptance or toleration of a relatively standardized product or at least a standardized set of components must be generated. A large demand will be needed to obtain the economies of scale. The resulting large demand can only be met initially by the government in its housing projects or by large private builders. One way to create acceptance of standardization is offered by the Proxmire Amendment (Section 108 of the Housing Act of 1968), which directs HUD to launch five projects of an experimental nature, each of which is to be built at the rate of 1,000 units a year for five years.

Although HUD was opposed to the passage of the Proxmire Amendment, apparently preferring to continue with its small-scale pilot projects, it is greatly to be hoped that the department will cooperate in this effort to create the large-scale market necessary to demonstrate the advantages of industrialized housing. The new administration will have the chance to galvanize the slow-moving bureaucracy into action.

It is this which Mayor Daley of Chicago is trying to carry out in cooperation with the unions and with National Homes in the initial installation of 200 prefabricated and sectionalized houses. Under this plan, a four-bedroom house plus an ample kitchen-dining room and a living room has been installed at a price of $14,500. This includes 1½ bathrooms, airconditioning, wall-to-wall carpeting, site improvements including trees, hedges, and lawn, and an individualized backyard plus a pooled patio for each unit of six houses. Each house is also equipped with good furniture purchased at factory prices. Such a house constructed by ordinary methods would cost from $22,000 to $24,000. Urban renewal land (generally vacant lots) is to be furnished at an additional cost of $1,500. The present houses are being manufactured at Lafayette, Indiana and are trucked to the site and then erected by a crane on a concrete base.

After the initial 200 units are installed and if they prove to be popular, a factory will be built in Chicago that will produce 2000 units a year on a one-shift basis. If demand permits, a second and third shift will also be employed. Financial institutions in Chicago are putting up one-third of the $2 million capital required for the factory, large-scale industries a third, and the craft unions the remaining third. The unions actually want to subscribe a larger amount.

In return, both the factory and the erection work will be conducted by union men; a large portion of the labor needed will be drawn from the unemployed of the neighborhood, and one business agent will represent both the carpenters and plumbers in their dealings with National Homes. It is fortunate that National Homes already has an excellent record of dealing cooperatively with the unions.

Interest of 1 percent will be charged each mortgage holder under the new Housing Act. Thus carrying charges will amount to $76 a month or $912 a year; which will make it possible for a large family with only a $3,600 income to purchase decent housing.

If nothing untoward develops, this is one of the most hopeful developments of recent years. It could only have been accomplished by a strong, public-spirited mayor with the power to waive unreasonable code and building requirements, and to get the support of labor, the banks and industry. Had political power been fragmented, conflicts of interest would probably have prevented any such agreement from being reached.

Other cities are preparing to follow in the wake of Chicago. All deserve the support of concerned citizens. For while we need subsidized housing for the poor, we also need lower building and operating costs both to reduce the subsidies needed and to make it possible for families with moderate incomes to buy or rent decent housing on a self-supporting basis.

If we can industrialize housing, new and better opportunities can be opened up both for living and for work. As we get away from the present limited market in housing we will break loose some of the barriers to the education and training of the young. However, to do this we will need initially large government subsidies to build for the poor, the near poor and the lower economic middle class.

(3) As government moves forward to assume the added responsibilities of providing housing for the poor, private industry should do likewise, and under the leadership of Henry Ford, a group of business leaders have pledged their help. A recent report indicates that up to the first of October, they had employed about 84,000 of the so-called "hard core" unemployed. They believed they would reach the 100,000 mark by the first of 1969 and had then set a target of 500,000 by 1971. Some subsidies should of course continue to be given as an inducement for private industry to hire the disadvantaged.

Ultimately, employment and training in private institutions should not take more than another $1½ billion a year.

The conventional means by which a man entered the skilled crafts, particularly the building trades, has in the past been through the institution of apprenticeship. However, the federal government has sought for years to systematize the training and conditions of work of the apprentices, and in the process has gathered statistics on apprenticeship. A summary of these is given in the accompanying table.

PROGRESS OF REGISTERED APPRENTICESHIP, 1941–1966
(in thousands)[a]

Year	Number of Apprentices in Training at End of Year	Number of New Registrations	Number of Cancellations	Number of Completions
1941	26.1	14.2	5.1	1.3
1946	131.2	84.7	8.4	2.0
1951	171.0	63.9	56.8	38.8
1956	188.1	74.1	33.4	27.2
1961	155.6	49.5	26.4	28.5
1962	158.9	55.6	26.4	25.9
1963	163.3	57.2	26.7	26.0
1964	170.5	60.0	27.0	25.7
1965	183.8	68.5	30.2	24.9
1966	207.5	85.0	34.9	26.5

a *Handbook of Labor Statistics*, 1968, Table 47, p. 93.

It is probable that the apparently large increase in the number of registered apprentices in the 1940's was primarily due to a better statistical coverage. From 1956 to 1965 there was no permanent increase in the total number although there was a distinct upward movement in 1966.

The high ratio of "cancellations," which are primarily, although not exclusively "dropouts," to "completions" is especially notable. In 1941 it was 4 to 1, as it was in 1946. In 1951, the ratio was nearly 1½ to 1. During the 1960's the number of cancellations only slightly exceeded the completions. The record has improved with the years. However, when it is realized that the period of apprenticeship generally lasts for several years and that the total cancellations over this period are therefore a multiple of the annual rate, it can be seen that for every apprentice who finishes his course and becomes a journeyman, several drop out along the way. To turn out around 25,000 journeymen a year is commendable, but it is obviously not an adequate answer to the widespread unemployment of slum youth.

For a long time, moreover, the selection of apprentices was largely a family affair. Trades were passed on from father to son or uncle to nephew. Where relationship was not the qualifying factor, family friendship often was. It was hard for outsiders to break in; this was especially true of the sons of poor families and markedly so if they were Negroes. When challenged on this score, the craftsmen could always make the retort that at the worst they were only doing what wealthy bankers, industrialists, and stock brokers had always done: namely, give favors to family and friends. The craftsmen inquire somewhat caustically why they should be expected to conform to a much higher standard of conduct than their critics. Within the last two years, however, there has been a distinct improvement in the methods of both selecting and training apprentices. Individuals are accepted by examination, and tutoring schools have been set up to prepare the relatively disadvantaged. Admission is far more open, and although racial discrimination is still present, it is far less common that it was. Progress has been made and, although it should be accelerated, it would be wrong to deny its existence.

It has become apparent, however, that supplements to the apprenticeship method must be developed. Senator Joseph Clark emphasized this from 1960 on and urged shorter courses, whether in training school or on the job, during which time the learner was to be paid maintenance allowances. Congress passed the Clark measure in 1962. During the next five years a total of nearly 800,-000 trainees were enrolled at a cost of approximately $1.2 billion. This was an average of about $1500 per person.

Of the total number enrolled, 600,000 or over 75 percent were trained in schools and 191,000 on the job. Sixty-two percent of the total were males but 38 percent were females, although it was harder to place the women with employers on the job. Sixty-eight percent of the trainees were white and 32 percent were Negroes. Again it was harder to place the Negroes for training on the job, where they formed only 24 percent of the total number as compared with the 35 percent of those who were being trained in and by institutions.[6]

Senator Clark had originally designed his bill not

6 *Handbook of Labor Statistics,* 1968, Table 48, p. 93.

only to cover the youngsters who had not yet found jobs but perhaps even more to help adults who had been squeezed out of previous jobs by automation or by a shifting of demand. Fifteen percent of the total trained or approximately 119,000 have been under the age of nineteen. Twenty-three percent or nearly 182,000 were in the age group from 19 to 21 years inclusive. This made a total of approximately 301,000 who were either juveniles or slightly older. Slightly over half of the total number or 52 percent were in the grouping from 21 to 44 years inclusive, and 11 percent or about 87,000 in all were over 45 years of age.

Of the 791,000 who had been enrolled during these five years, 468,000 or about 60 percent finished their training. Of these, 366,000 obtained a job or were employed at the time the last contact was made with them, which was 46 percent of the number who started. This may be something of an understatement, for some of those who started had not had time to finish their training and therefore could not have been expected to find work. A more precise index is perhaps that 78 percent of those who successfully completed their training had found a job.

It will be remembered that there were two methods of training, the first in schools, whether trade or commercial, and the second on the job itself. Success seems to have been somewhat better with the latter method than with the former. For the period as a whole, 94,000 or 49 percent of the 191,000 who were trained on the job found a job as compared with 45 percent of those who were trained in a school. The average cost per student placed was $2,100 for those who were trained on the job as compared with $3,500 for those who were trained in school. The Department of Labor therefore decided to lay its emphasis more on job than school training, but the difficulty was in finding enough employers who would be willing to take on subsidized youngsters for training.

Although the failures and drop outs in any system of training are numerous and there are many discouragements, the program is thoroughly worthwhile. It deserves increased support, for it helps to transform men and their families from being economic liabilities to society into economic assets, and from being "tax-eaters," as they are sometimes brutally called, into tax producers. Even more important, it gives each worker a sense of self-respect when he finishes his training and gets a foothold on life in some specific job. It is important however to raise the percentage of those who successfully finish their training and of those who, having done so, find employment.

What should be done to care for those who fail, or even worse for those who do not really try, is a question to which society has given no clear answer. Thus it is frequently objected that extensive training programs will not be effective on the ground that the young unemployed have been so demoralized by unemployment and poverty that they do not want either to work or to train. This is probably true of a certain percentage, as all readers of Oscar Lewis' *The Children of Sanchez* and *La Vida* are forced to admit. How large this group is, no one can estimate with any accuracy. The point is that this tendency is not universal and that there is certainly

a proportion of the group whom expanded voluntary programs would attract, and therefore the programs have
been enlarged by one of the 1967 amendments to the
Social Security Act, which provides for either work or
training for those who are able. Also, the 1967 amendments require that boys and girls 16 and 17 years of age,
who are now on AFDC, take either a job or training,
which will be referred to them by the public employment
agencies. If they refuse, the welfare payments are to be
shut off. If they accept, then a training allowance will be
given and those who get jobs can keep the first $30 of
their monthly pay plus a third of their earnings above
this without any deduction from their welfare allowances.
The federal government will meet 80 percent of the
costs of this program with the state and local governments each contributing 10 percent. Authorizations have
been approved for 8400 grants in New York City and
12,000 for the State of New York. This plan has been
accepted by both Governor Rockefeller and Mayor Lind-
say. On the basis of the New York figures, it would seem
that a corresponding figure for the country as a whole
would not be far from 100,000 if the localities will only
cooperate.

Although the amendment covers others beside the
16- and 17-year-olds, it can have a greater effect on this
group because the young have far fewer disabilities and
obligations to keep them at home. Would it be excessive
to hope that at least 75,000 of this age group could be
reached initially by this program? This would be about
one-fifth of the 400,000 youths of both sexes in this age
group who were listed as being unemployed in 1967.

Because the number of children under 18 receiving aid in June of 1968 amounted to 4.2 million, it seems that the 16-to-17 group on welfare probably amounted to somewhat more than this.

I personally see little reason why at least two-thirds to three-quarters of these youths should not be given an alternative to work or learn and that while the stick is held in reserve, the carrot should be stressed initially.

III

Let us, however, face facts which liberal-spirited men and women have generally been unwilling to consider. There will be a considerable number of youngsters who are so ruined from the use of drugs and alcohol and from their continued antisocial behavior and lack of work that they cannot be redeemed or transformed into useful citizens. There is and will be human wastage. What shall the community do with them? One school advocates our leaving them strictly alone. Here they would not receive public charity but would be forced to rely on private gifts and intermittent work. There is something to be said for this as a policy in the case of the so-called "beatniks," "hippies," and "yippies." The difficulty with it is that while society might not interfere with them, they would be constantly interfering with society. There would be assaults, thefts, armed robberies, civil riots, arson, and on occasion murders. Even in a generally humane social order, these forms of antisocial behavior would continue although, I believe, in a greatly reduced volume. Society cannot however tolerate such direct crimes against it.

If we provide helpful justice and compassion, we are then certainly entitled to impose law and to try to create order. The punishment involved should be swift and sure but need not be excessively severe. The newer penologists such as Thomas Mott Osborne and James Bennett have shown us a better way. Outdoor camps of correction can be used for the young offenders while useful employment indoors can be given to the older ones. I was much impressed two years ago by a visit to the new high security prison in Southern Illinois which replaced the former notorious Alcatraz. No one there was in prison dress. All were busy at useful tasks. There was an air of cheerfulness and of honest effort about the place. And there had been no attempt at a jail break and no assault on the guards. If men like the ones running this prison can be put in charge of our penal institutions, they might indeed become places of correction. Is this, too, an impossible hope?

Meanwhile, I believe we should continue with such useful programs as Head Start, the Neighborhood Youth Corps, and the Job Corps. I submit that on balance they have been useful and productive. The newer programs I urge, even if adopted, will not meet all the needs, and they will need to be supplemented. If not adopted or only partially carried out, there are other programs such as the maintainance of income that will be all the more required. However, I favor the more positive efforts at training and employment rather than a merely passive provision of income to those who choose to remain idle.

We have some deep and subborn problems of race and poverty in this country that have been coming to a climax in our cities. They cannot be neglected nor easily and inexpensively improved. They will need both effort and money.

IV

There was once a Congressman who after every appropriation was authorized or approved, would rise from his seat and shout, "Where are you going to get the money?" Although such a cry grew somewhat monotonous over the years, it nevertheless posed an important question, which the advocates of social reform should not only consider but for which they should have some appropriate answers.

The measures which I have outlined for training and employment would probably cost close to $5 billion a year. However, a large amount of money, no one can say how much, would be saved in the reduction of relief, riots, crime, and punishment. Further amounts would be gained from an increase in earning power that would create employment elsewhere and help offset the costs of the programs. But here again there are no hard figures to support one's faith.

We believe it would be a productive investment and that the money needed could be obtained from a number of sources.

(1) One source would be the increase in governmental revenues caused by an increase in the national income. During the last eight years, the gross national product in terms of dollars of constant purchasing power has increased by a total of $225 billion, or an average yearly increase of about $28 billion. The increase in the GNP during the third quarter of 1968 was at a yearly rate which, in terms of current dollars, was $37 billion above the corresponding quarter of 1967. Because federal tax receipts have amounted to about one-sixth of the GNP this would mean that there has been a normal annual growth of between $5 and $6 billion in receipts with no alteration in tax rates. What is wrong with using economic growth to subsidize human growth?

(2) With the probable diminution in the scale and intensity of the war in Vietnam, it should be possible to divert a respectable proportion of the war expenditures now amounting to $30 or $35 billion a year to purposes of peace and social reconstruction.

(3) Certain civilian expenditures can and should be reduced if we were only bold enough to establish a proper system of priorities. Should we spend $5 billion a year on going to the moon and the planets? Should we heavily subsidize the supersonic airplane so that the jet set may save three hours in getting to the hot spots in Soho and Paris? Do we need to spend $5½ billion annually on our super highways? Should we give billions to wealthy farmers as a reward for their decreasing production?

(4) If we could plug some of the many loopholes in our federal tax system in the form of unneeded depletion allowances, untaxed capital gains, unreported interest and dividends, and other special privileges, we could also save many billions of dollars a year.

(5) Is it impossible that the American public might sometime realize that from 1956 to 1966, the bare land

values of the country increased by about $250 billion, or from $270 to $520 billion? This was neither an earning nor a stealing. It was in fact a simple finding, caused primarily by the increase in population and in productivity. It was primarily created by society. Would it not be proper therefore for society to take at least a portion of this gain to help finance the expenditures that have been necessitated by many of those same social developments which have enriched the owners of land? Are these facts always to be sidetracked by the derisive remark, "Oh, that is Henry George" or "That's the single tax," as though to label them was to refute them?

Can we seriously tackle the problems of opening up useful careers for the young and be resolved to meet them?

THE ROLE OF GOVERNMENT IN IMPROVING THE URBAN ENVIRONMENT

Robert C. Weaver

THE SUBJECT OF THIS PAPER, the role of government in bettering our urban environment, has two basic aspects. The first relates to the functions that public agencies perform in urban America. The second deals with the allocation of these functions among different levels of government and the relationship among these levels.

At the outset, I want to outline briefly the role I see for government in bettering the urban environment. I am convinced that there is little option as to whether or not government will be involved. It is involved, and it will, of necessity, continue to be involved. The issues before us, therefore, are questions about the degree of this involvement and the methods utilized by government in achieving its purposes.

In a mixed economy such as ours, government involvement does not mean preemption of the field by public agencies. Rather it leads to, and requires, a joint

effort, involving all levels of government, private organizations, private industry, and, most recently, neighborhood groups.

There will, of course, continue to be colloquy relative to the degree of governmental participation in urban
matters. Interestingly enough, in all probability, necessity and unsolved problems, more than philosophy, will
determine the intensity and the directions of the involvement. Political ideology may temporarily dictate new
emphasis and priorities, but these, too, ultimately will
be determined by what an urban people recognizes as its
needs and aspires to achieve. Thus to delineate problems
on a case by case basis is, in my opinion, the most rewarding approach to the subject before us.

I

In recent years the semantic at the national level has
assumed public involvement in urban matters and
concentrated upon discussing means of effecting a partnership between public and private resources and institutions. Thus, the Johnson administration has involved
private enterprise, private entrepreneurship, and private
finance to an unprecedented degree in urban renewal,
housing, employment, and job training. An indispensable
characteristic of this involvement is that it is made viable
by a series of public subsidies that render it possible to
achieve social goals and still yield a profit to the private
sponsor or investor.

During the period when tax concessions *and* subsidies were successfully combined to produce lower-

income housing, there have been, and are, those who would place full reliance upon tax incentives. Herein lies a basic issue. Can government achieve, largely through tax incentives, our urban goals and our social purposes without additional public support? I think not.

By way of illustration, let us consider the difficult problems of housing for low- and moderate-income families. The means of achieving innovation in controversial fields is to add the new without simultaneously destroying the old. There are several reasons for this. The new is untried; and until it is proved, destruction of current programs would be imprudent. Then, too, every existing program has its proponents, many of whom have strong vested interests in its perpetuation, and the new proposal is sure to invite their opposition. A legislative strategy to be successful would not arouse that opposition by threatening its projects at the time it is proposing a new approach.

In the struggle to secure enactment of the rent supplement program, for example, we took special pains not to propose it as a substitute for public housing. The strategy of the administration was to present the two programs as complementary, noting that together they were still insufficient to meet the total need. However, in the Congress, some of the proponents of the new approach claimed that it would replace public housing; others expressed the fear that such a substitution might occur as a basis for their opposition.

Interestingly enough, each approach involved a form of public subsidy. The public housing approach requires annual contributions from the federal government to pay the debt service on the capital cost. Likewise rents are reduced by virtue of tax-exempt, local-authority bond financing and partial exemption from property taxes by local government. Sponsorship, planning, supervision of construction, and management are carried out by a local public agency. Private enterprise is involved only through the bidding and building phases of the process.

Several years ago HUD initiated a new approach to public housing, identified as "Turnkey." Under Turnkey, a private builder proposes a site, develops architectural plans, and supervises and carries out the construction. When the structures are completed and accepted by the local housing authority, the private developer turns the key over to the local agency—thus the name Turnkey.

In the case of rent supplements, the role of private enterprise is greater, but there is a basic public involvement. Private sponsors plan, construct, manage, and own these developments. There are three types of sponsors, limited dividend, nonprofit, and cooperatives. In all types of sponsorship, the difference between "economic rents" [1] and rents low-income families can afford is made up by a federally contributed supplement paid to the sponsor. Limited dividend sponsors are restricted to a profit of no more than 6 percent on their equity investment. They find the programs attractive because of the tax shelter that rapid depreciation affords them.

The Housing Act of 1961 authorized the first national moderate-income housing program. As with the subse-

---

1 Economic rents are the rent figures that would cover all operating costs, depreciation, amortization of debt, and yield a competitive profit.

quently developed rent supplements, this moderate-income program was restricted to limited dividend, nonprofit, and cooperative sponsors. The gap between economic rents and the rent the tenant could pay was compensated for by a submarket interest rate. Thus, there was an interest subsidy, and the incentives for the limited dividend sponsors were a 6 percent return on equity, tax shelter benefits, as well as equity accumulation through amortization.

Interest-rate subsidies also were provided in the Housing and Urban Development Act of 1968. The moderate-income rental and cooperative program was modified by establishing a flexible interest-rate subsidy which was adjusted to permit effective rates as low as 1 per cent. In addition, a home ownership program for lower-income families was added. It involved a similar interest-rate subsidy but was made available to profit-oriented as well as limited and nonprofit builders.

Clearly all of these approaches to low- and moderate-income housing need to be consolidated. Now that they are a reality, it is possible to plan for consolidating the approaches without sacrificing any of the unique benefits of each. Initial steps in this direction already are under way. The 1961 moderate-income program will soon be phased out and replaced by the 1968 rental program. Simultaneously, developments initiated under the first program are being converted to the second, for it is necessary to have operating experience in order to establish criteria by which the process can be carried out. Some of the possible criteria for consolidation which suggest themselves are grouping tenants according to their

income or consolidating projects according to the nature
of the sponsor or public agency. At first blush, neither of
these appears to be satisfactory. If the first is selected,
our current efforts toward mixing income groups as much
as possible is vitiated. If the second is accepted, there will
still be two programs dealing exclusively with low-
income housing, often in the same locality. Perhaps the
answer will be to consolidate all of these activities into a
single administrative unit.

As we have moved more boldly toward cooperation
between government and private enterprise in providing
low- and moderate-income housing, certain principles
become apparent. First, federal involvement in this partnership is not beamed exclusively at economic ends.
Equally—and often more important—are the social goals.
Establishment of national priorities and utilization of
resources for specific purposes are fundamental and
often unique functions of the federal government.

Second, if private investment and involvement are to
be enlisted, they must be provided with a profit. If there
is to be significant involvement, the return must be
competitive, with allowance for the degree of risk. Where
rental housing is involved, care must be taken to guard
against the owners' charging higher rents for greater earnings alone. Where publicly assisted housing is provided,
steps need to be taken to see that the housing is not over-
priced in terms of its value and that it is within the
means of those for whom it was intended.

By restricting sponsorship for rental housing to
limited dividend and nonprofit developers, it is assured
that they cannot charge higher rentals for higher earn-

ings. The provision of loans to home buyers that cannot exceed all of a very high proportion of the FHA-appraised value of the home and careful review of architectural plans provide safeguards for lower-income purchasers against higher prices.

A combination of limiting the return on his investment and tax benefits yields a net return to the investor of from 13 to 16 per cent if the building is owned for 10 years and sold. At the same time, the interest rate, or (in the case of rent supplements) direct subsidies make the developments viable. These subsidies, when combined with the housing needs of a large number of poorly housed households, assure an adequate demand and flow of rental income. In economic terms, these subsidies—the public contribution—make a need of great magnitude an effective demand. Without such an effective demand, there would be either insufficient rental income to support the development or the housing would be priced beyond the paying abilities of lower-income households.

Tax concessions alone are not sufficient to support low-income housing. Indeed, if government is to be a creative partner in urban housing, it must take special care to be more than a dispenser of boodle. Its assistance should be so directed and so protected as to provide a decent return to the private investor but also assure a benefit that has high social value.

Our experience indicates that existing tax concessions are of sufficient magnitude to attract a significant and an increasing number of qualified limited dividend housing sponsors. The economics of this are simple. Because of the great need, which translates families into potential renters, and the subsidy, which translates need into rent paying ability, the market is greatly expanded. The same applies to houses built for sale. What was formerly a high-risk market becomes one of lower risk. It is also a volume market, reducing the period for renting or selling.

This analysis of housing for lower-income households is instructive because it pinpoints a basic issue in the role of the federal government in urban affairs. It is presented to suggest—indeed affirm—that in low- and moderate-income housing, there must be government assistance. However, it goes further and attempts to demonstrate that simply to provide higher and higher tax incentives is not enough. Rather a combination of subsidy and tax concessions is the best approach in a socio-economic context. The former renders the latter effective, while avoiding an increase in tax benefits and assuring that the developments will be both economically sound and responsive to the needs and requirements of less affluent people.

II

Lower-income housing programs present another complicated issue of public policy. In recent years, there has been great pressure for involvement in these activities, especially by ghetto residents. However, if we have learned anything, it is that the more sophisticated and better financed limited-dividend sponsors can build more units more quickly than most nonprofit groups can. If a larger volume of construction, quickly initiated and rapidly completed, is our goal, the limited-dividend entrepreneur is by far the most effective sponsor.

At the same time, the emerging black power movement is pressing for "a piece of the action"—or for the entire action. The rhetoric varies. Some of it demands total concentration on developing entrepreneurship within the ghetto. This is green power. Some of it is an expression of antiwhite attitudes. The ghetto, it is said, should be rebuilt exclusively by black men and by black businesses. This attitude holds that white ownership in the ghetto is a continuation of exploitative imperialism.

In the world of reality, as contrasted to the world of rhetoric, the situation is more complex. Because of centuries of discrimination and institutionalized color patterns, both in finance and the building trades, there are few ghetto businessmen who now have the capital, capacity, and experience to compete effectively for this type of work. The few who have the capacity usually operate on a limited scale. That means that if construction is delayed while a new segment of entrepreneurship is developed, thousands of nonwhite families would have to wait, perhaps a long time, for better housing.

In this colloquy, as with so many issues affecting the ghetto, there is a tendency to polarize—to speak in terms of "either-or" alternatives. However, I do not see the improvement of living conditions inside the ghetto as the creation of a gilded ghetto, *provided that internal improvements are made together with successful efforts to*

*remove the barriers that confine people to segregated
areas.* Without both internal ghetto improvements and
external mobility, there is no true solution.

The same applies to the matter of entrepreneurship.
Housing is needed—now. We must use the tools that will
provide the maximum volume of housing for low- and
moderate-income households as quickly as possible. This
means using all the sponsorship forms currently available. However, we must also encourage and aid the
development of effective black entrepreneurship, too.
Also we need to encourage nonprofit and cooperative
sponsors, in part to stimulate ownership and citizen involvement.

Government should be concerned with using new
financial tools in the ghetto, not only as instruments for
training and employing craftsmen, but also for training
the entrepreneur and teaching management skills. Instruments have already been created which will facilitate
this. The first is the Model Cities program, and the second
is assistance to nonprofit sponsors of low- and moderate-
income housing provided in the 1968 act. A third is the
work of the Small Business Administration, supported by
administrative action of FHA.

Under the Model Cities program we anticipate a
scale and scope of construction and reconstruction that
will challenge the capacity of existing resources. We
must, therefore, develop new and heretofore undeveloped
resources.

It is possible to use Model City funds to develop new
enterpreneurs and managers, as well as craftsmen and
mechanics. I expect that in many cities the funds will be

so used. It is my belief, too, that in most model cities, where planning will include the people in the affected neighborhoods, so that they will develop a better understanding of available alternatives, there will emerge a demand for a balanced housing program. This will facilitate both rapid upgrading of shelter and significant training in all phases of housing planning, sponsorship, production, and management.

The new Housing and Urban Development Act authorizes HUD to provide information, advice, and technical assistance with respect to the construction, rehabilitation, and operation of low- and moderate-income housing sponsored by nonprofit organizations. It also authorizes 80 percent interest-free loans to these organizations.

Concurrently, the Small Business Administration is developing programs to provide financial and technical assistance to Negro builders. FHA is aiding by modifying its bonding requirements.

Thus the federal role, as reflected in current programs, is one of rapidly expanding the housing supply for lower-income households, encouraging and aiding development of entrepreneurship in the ghetto, and providing technical and financial assistance to nonprofit sponsors.

At the same time, the federal government is devising new instruments to encourage greater participation by profit-oriented sponsors. The new forms of financing low- and moderate-income housing are a part of this activity, as is the Turnkey approach to public housing. A most recent element in this effort is the National Housing Partnership authorized in the 1968 act. This is designed to create a new partnership between private enterprise and government, so that this nation can turn its industrial might to the housing dilemmas of poor Americans. The partnership will provide for pooling of investments, spreading of risks, and development of management skills. It can create many different kinds of joint housing ventures in cities and thus help American labor provide new job opportunities to those blocked from earning a decent living. It can pour a vast managerial potential— resident in large corporations—into a myriad of housing efforts, many of them government supported, to help those without decent shelter.

The creation of such an instrument is, in my opinion, a proper and highly desirable activity of the federal government.

III

The problems and programs discussed above are but a part of a much larger problem. It relates to the total shelter requirements of the years ahead. And that, in turn, is but one aspect of urban development.

The issues involved are both quantitative and qualitative. The quantitative issue is over how to provide for a rapidly increasing population. There will be some 40 million more Americans in 1980 than there are now. They would fill eighty cities the size of Denver. However, whether Americans live in small towns, new towns, suburbs, or cities, they are going to demand—at the very minimum—a staggering amount of what urbanists call "infrastructure": schools, streets, sewers, electric lines. They will need jobs, and homes, as well as food, clothing, and medical care.

The ten-year housing goal of the 1968 Housing and Urban Development Act postulates the construction of 26 million dwelling units, six million of them subsidized for low- and moderate-income occupancy. To meet the goal for subsidized housing alone will require an annual volume of subsidized construction ten times greater than that of the last ten years. To achieve housing production on a scale responsive to the needs of all Americans means overcoming a number of traditional constraints: an inadequate supply of trained labor, a periodically in-adequate flow of mortgage financing, a lack of sites for subsidized housing, a fragmented building industry. It means modifying institutional impediments: zoning and taxation policies, building codes, inflexible labor union regulations, governmental red tape. And it calls for a sustained and well-financed program of research and development.

The quantitative issues are no greater than those involving quality and equity. In the broadest sense, resolution of the urban crisis turns on resolving problems of poverty, race, citizen participation, proliferation of local governments, and municipal finance. Putting a floor under income (especially for those with incomes too low even for our subsidized programs), breaking segregated residential patterns, increasing the citizen's role in decision-making, developing more effective instruments of local government, providing tax-sharing or some other form of substantial financial aid to local governments—

these are some of the major issues that the nation must tackle.

Taking these issues in specific terms, one of the first things to learn is how to build in controls which go beyond mere concern for volume of construction. By this I mean assuring good land use and better design; the balanced development, with a retention of free mobility, of inner-city and suburb; genuine equal access for all Americans; and improved management of multifamily developments.

Each of these issues merits detailed analysis. Rather than attempting such a comprehensive presentation here, I shall select several which are both immediate and crucial, asserting that government—the federal government, in particular—has a role in dealing with each of them.

It is obvious that if we are to achieve the goal of 26 million housing starts over the next decade with 6 million for low- and moderate-income families, there must be adequate financing. For the 6 million subsidized units, this requires appropriations for subsidies, as well as private mortgage credit.

For the subsidized housing and the remaining 20 million units, there must be a steadily increasing volume of mortgage money. To secure this flow, three things are necessary:

(1) An adequate and assured secondary market on which mortgages can be traded.

(2) Instruments for tapping new sources of investment capital for mortgages.

(3) Governmental policy—at the federal level—to

encourage and facilitate an adequate supply of mortgage credit, especially during relatively full employment and tight-money periods.

Action was taken in 1968 to convert the FNMA to a government-sponsored private corporation. This will take secondary market mortgage operations out of the budget, thus relieving the volume of such activity from budgetary restrictions. This secondary market will have access to greater resources, and its operations can and should be more responsive to the credit requirements of housing construction.

Simultaneously, the newly created GNMA, a government corporation, is authorized to guarantee securities backed by mortgages or loans insured or guaranteed by FHA, VA, or the Farmers Home Administration. Because the new securities will be in large denominations issued for specific and variable periods and will not require the servicing of many individual mortgages, they are expected to attract mortgage funding from a new group of investors. Their principal target will be the pension funds, the assets of which continue to grow rapidly.

These two developments should bring a greater amount and a larger proportion of investment funds into mortgages. However, they will not solve the problem of the periodic shortage of such funds. In times of tight money, the mortgage market is adversely affected early and usually with peculiar intensity. Government has a basic role to play in this situation. First, of course, its economic policies should encourage continuing economic growth. Second, it has a responsibility to arrange its fiscal and monetary policies so that the financing of housing will not experience a disporportionate share of the so-called "credit crunch."

Traditionally, the fate of the flow of credit into mortgages is a result of budgetary, fiscal, and monetary decisions. If we are to achieve our housing goals, this cannot be allowed to continue. The federal government must place a high priority on activity in housing construction and weigh the desirability of budgetary, fiscal, and monetary actions against their impact on housing.

There is no avenue of escape for the federal government. If it fails to assume a positive position and ignores the peculiar requirements of the mortgage market, it is playing a role. It is a role of countenancing periodic starvation of funds to finance construction, and the consequence will be chronic or periodic shortages of shelter.

IV

A nation that is to double its population in less than half a century is concerned about land as well as people. Despite the fact that only 1 percent of our land is used for urban living, and by the early twenty-first century only 2 percent will be so used, we have urban land-use problems.

The essence of urban life is a concentration of people in a limited area. Although new communities are an exciting prospect, most of our new population growth will be contiguous to existing cities and suburbs. The question remains how this growing urbanization will occur. It could take place as more uncoordinated, haphazard scattering that will waste valuable land, complicate transportation, involve unnecessary and uneconomic expenditures for facilities, and duplicate the worst features of current suburbia.

The other alternative requires an awareness of land use, a concern for preserving open space and developing effective patterns of site development. In brief, it recognizes that man should and can control his physical environment and develop rational spatial arrangements.

When the average citizen drives in America, observing the broad expanses of space, land use does not seem to be a pressing problem. Only after he moves out of the city and is still harassed by rush-hour traffic congestion, and initially exposed to wells that are dry and septic tanks that are wet, does he recognize that land-use patterns are important to him. Subsequently, when he discovers the cost of community water and sewer systems and the impossibility of mass transit in a scattered community, he may wonder if unplanned urban land uses are acceptable.

The developer faces these issues much earlier, for he must consider land cost. During the last decade he has seen the price of land increase more rapidly than any other major component in the cost of new housing. He may resist the notion of a public policy affecting urban land use, but he is apprehensive lest he price himself out of the market.

The truth of the matter is that although we have long been an urban nation, we do not have an urban land policy. And in this respect we are unique among the economically advanced countries.

Urban land use in this nation is haphazard and

usually unplanned. The price of urban land usually reflects little input by the owner but rather the presence of people and expenditures for public improvements and services. At present, standards of design for urban development depend upon decisions of thousands of entrepreneurs who act independently. They are often motivated by an urge to maximize profits as quickly as possible. They face zoning ordinances that too frequently inhibit good design and efficient land use.

The need for an urban land policy is clear. Its roots are the requirements of a rapidly urbanizing society. It calls for recognition of the key role of planning and the initiation of new policies. One which seems obvious is some program for advanced acquisition of land for urban development. This will involve the optioning or purchasing of land now unused, or in agricultural use, but clearly destined for urbanization in a few years or a few decades.

Advanced acquisition of land for urban development by state or local agencies would not only facilitate land use controls but also come to grips with the matter of land price. By optioning or purchasing sites for urban expansion beforehand, speculative increases in land prices can be avoided and the cost of shelter can be reduced. The increase in land value, created primarily by social and public action, would be passed on to the people who have created, and will create, it. At the same time, the cost to the taxpayers for building schools and other public facilities, and preserving open space, would be appreciably lessened.

Though logical and economically sound, this proposal faces many difficulties. The first is our long tradition of land tenure, nurtured in an agricultural past and basic to our disposition of federal lands. The second is our general attitude toward land—an attitude which Marion Clausen has aptly described as "the idea of unrestricted land ownership." This laissez-faire concept not only militates against public acquisition or optioning of land, but also greatly weakens the scope and efficacy of planning in this nation.

The federal role is one of setting standards, articulating objectives, and providing inducements to the states to plan future land use. But time is running out. We should at once start the discussion, develop the programs, and begin the colloquy. If we fail to face up to this issue, we shall, by default, create unnecessary problems for our progeny—problems that they will have to face but will find complicated and unnecessarily expensive if we are negligent.

One aspect of land use is rarely identified as such. It relates to the possibility and desirability of continuing the concentration of nonwhites in the central cities and providing employment for them in the same sector of urban America. The issue is usually presented as a matter of philosophy and desirability. Seldom are its economics considered.

Regardless of one's dedication to integration or ethnic concentration, it is impossible to conceive of accommodating the present ghetto residents and the natural increase of that population within its present confines. For we must recognize that the Negro and Spanish-American urban population is composed of an abnormally large number of persons with a high child-bearing potential and achievement.

Additional space will have to be found; otherwise densities will become so high as to threaten housing standards and complicate the provision of adequate facilities and services.

At the same time, there is a question of employment. Current trends are for blue collar jobs, especially, to be moved out of central cities into the suburbs. Failure of minorities to gain access to nearby housing has been a serious impediment to their employment.

As with shelter, the ghetto, even if expanded, cannot and will not provide anything approaching the job opportunities required by its present residents. For a short time rehabilitation and rebuilding of ghetto areas can and should provide construction and other types of work, but if the reconstruction is done properly, it will not be a repetitive effort. The increase in work will be a short-run phenomenon. Over the long-run most of the construction and other workers will have to seek employment beyond the confines of the ghetto.

Thus, we must look for housing sites for low- and moderate-income families outside as well as inside the ghettos and central cities. This will present problems. A viable urban land policy, effectively administered, would enable us to deal more effectively with this crucial issue; the Civil Rights Act of 1968 sets forth an enlightened national policy to encourage and require open occupancy.

The issues discussed above are typical of the problems that government must face. In these, as in all problems of urbanization, the central government is a partner, developing national objectives and goals, providing financial support and technical assistance, and adjusting its other activities to promote the achievement of a better urban environment. In this partnership there is a varied mix. Private enterprise, various levels of government, and a combination of the two are called for. The challenge for the future is to determine the best combination of each and to perfect techniques to make the joint effort more responsive to the needs of urban America.

There are still other basic roles for the federal government. Laws and public programs are the result of the consent of the governed. In order that such consent may be enlightened, it must be recognized that most issues involve more than being for or against public action. Issues need to be delineated, solutions need to be formulated, and truly viable choices must be presented. The voter needs sophistication if he is to express effectively his consent or his opposition.

V

Although the preceding discussion has been oriented principally to the role of the federal government, it has, of necessity, also involved references to functions and responsibilities of state and local governments. Repeatedly I have spoken of partnerships between levels of government in the area of urban problem solving.

Actually, there is much greater understanding and agreement as to the role of local government than there is of state government. Most Americans accept the principle that the local government, because it is closest to the people, should take the initiative in planning and carrying out programs that affect local citizens. In light of financial reality, it is also generally recognized that the federal government should assist in paying for certain locally directed functions. The bone of contention is the degree to which federal money brings federal control.

As a general principle, we have developed a concept of local initiation, development, and operation—limited, however, by federal program requirements and federal review and evaluation of performance. Although this approach is frequently attacked by local government and others as involving red tape, it is in accord with our tradition of checks and balances. The local initiation and local operational responsibility prevent the federal bureaucracy from operating and controlling programs (and local government). They also, of course, permit the degree of flexibility in operations that a large and diversified nation requires. At the same time, federal requirements and standards, as well as federal review of achievements and expenditures, provide protection against local abuses. What we have is a system that shares authority and thereby, it is assumed, avoids the excesses and abuses of undivided authority.

Although such an approach is somewhat cumbersome and subject to constant criticism, especially on the part of those who feel its constraints, it has worked fairly well. The proof of this lies in the constantly increasing number of new programs of federal aid to cities sought by localities and enacted by the Congress. However, it is this very apparent success that has made the system cumbersome, for as the programs proliferate, a system, tolerable for a limited number of activities, becomes administratively burdensome.

That I believe is the situation today, and it finds expression in the criticism of the hundreds of grants and loan programs that are currently available. The issue is further complicated by the fact that not only have these programs proliferated, but they are administered by scores of federal departments and independent agencies. Their impact is not always a consistent one, and their diversified administrative requirements place a real burden upon local officials.

The suggestion most often proposed to cure this situation is that revenue should be shared to some extent by different levels of government, perhaps in the form of block grants. Although there is no question in my mind that we must consolidate federal aid to our urban areas, I am not yet convinced that block grants, with a minimum of federal control and supervision, are either universally desirable or politically possible.

The advocates of block grants are not a homogeneous group, nor are those who speak for urban interests necessarily the most powerful. Indeed, I suspect that the most influential advocates of block grants are those who propose that federal assistance be channeled directly to the states. As urbanists recognize this, their enthusiasm for block grants, *per se*, weakens. At the least, they want their kind of block grants—those which go directly from the federal government to the cities.

As this thinking becomes more sophisticated, some of the urban proponents of block grants are questioning if such grants can be separated from the campaign to feed all federal aid through the states. If the answer is in the negative, urbanists have little choice. They must find other instruments to achieve their objectives. The reason is simple and its root is the traditional neglect of, or discrimination against, urban areas by state governments.

There is a more basic issue. It is whether or not the federal requirements can be so generalized that they can be set forth in terms that would apply to a cluster of activities. Clearly, if such requirements need to be tailor made for special activities, the categorical rather than the block-grant approach is suggested. Few informed persons would question that where federal funds are involved such federal policies as nondiscrimination must be required. However, in the instance of programs that can affect people, and where there may be strong economic planning, or even special interest forces pressing for specific goals not oriented towards people, we may ask if a federally financed program can avoid involvement in program direction or early concern for detailed program results.

Urban renewal affords an interesting example. In an effort to restore and revitalize core areas and strengthen the economic base of the central cities, this program concentrated upon total clearance, production of middle- and higher-income housing, and redevelopment of central retail and commercial businesses. In the process, relocation was badly done, people were dislocated from familiar neighborhoods, and little low- or moderate-income housing was provided. In addition, because of the starvation of the program in the mid and late 1950's, localities began to accumulate large grant reservations without moving the program.

Since 1961, HHFA and HUD have, through new legislation and a great deal of administrative action, begun to change the nature of urban renewal—largely by humanizing it.

Total clearance is deemphasized and rehabilitation is facilitated wherever possible. Through a series of new legislative provisions and certain administrative requirements, low- and moderate-income housing is being built on urban renewal sites. A balanced program, involving more rehabilitation, a smaller amount of total clearance, and more and more low- and moderate-income shelter is emerging.

Relocation has become a principal concern of the federal agencies involved, so that much more generous benefits are offered those to be dislocated. More important, the federal government has progressively raised relocation standards, upgraded the efficacy of their enforcement, and required greater local efforts to inform those affected of their rights. In some instances it has been necessary to hold up activity in local urban renewal programs because of failures in the relocation process.

By setting up administratively a system of priorities to govern the operation of urban renewal, the federal government has been able to assure that it is no longer a program that tears down housing occupied by the poor and constructs in its place housing for the affluent. Through administrative action, HUD was able to recapture hundreds of millions of dollars which were being frozen in localities lacking either the drive or ability to utilize them effectively.

The basic problem is how to maintain the capacity for such socially desirable controls and, at the same time, abandon categorical grants. The situation is akin to that involved in relying for the most part on tax concessions as a means of financing urban programs, a means too loose to be really efficient. It is difficult to estimate in advance what the cost of tax concessions will be to the government, nor does it, in or by itself, necessarily lead to the accomplishment of the social goals which was its *raison d'être*. Similarly, block grants, in certain types of activities, may or may not further the announced goal, and in the process they may create side effects that prove to be unduly oppressive to elements in society which are, in fact, least able to absorb the costs.

This then suggests that experimentation with block grants should be carried out on a selected basis. It would be prudent to start with the least complicated programs where it is possible to set simple performance standards, and where uncomplicated criteria and effective post audit can be devised. Out of that experience, it may be that techniques for more widespread applicability can be developed.

But there is still another impediment. Legislation and appropriations come out of committees and sub-committees in the Congress. Each is jealous of its jurisdiction; each identifies with the programs it facilitates. The grouping of programs in block grants would, I suspect, occasion political problems unless it was done with great skill.

VI

The call for further involvement of states in urban affairs comes from many quarters. The most positive manifestations of this emanate from New York and New Jersey. Some promising beginnings are being made in other parts of the country. Both New York and New Jersey are developing positive programs with capable staffs and providing financial support for their activities. In most instances, however, the current version of the old "states rights" plea is that federal grants to cities be passed through the states rather than directly to the urban areas. There is little inclination on the part of those who advocate this negative role to provide more than a transmittal line and state control. The missing ingredient is some form of state financial assistance. In view of the short-changing and insensitivity to their problems which the larger urban communities have traditionally received from state governments, it is understandable that the cities are unenthusiastic about this prospect.

However, there is a pressing need for state involvement. It should not be a sterile injection of another layer of bureaucracy that makes no positive contribution. Rather it should be an involvement that channels resources, on an equitable basis, to urban communities, or one that deals with problems which the states are uniquely capable of handling. The financial bind all cities face is clear justification for the first proposal of augmenting resources where the need is great and pressing. The second proposal of providing assistance which the states have a unique capacity to perform merits further delineation.

Because the states have all the powers they have not relinquished either to the federal government or local governments, they still retain enormous authority. The number and diversity of states, as contrasted to a single national government, make them less feared as a source of central control and more flexible in program development. Thus there are a series of crucial roles that the states can and should perform.

Reference was made earlier to the need for an urban land policy in the United States. The responsibility of the federal government to take leadership in its development and provide financial assistance for its execution was also set forth. However, both because of our systems and structure of government, as well as our traditions, the states are the units of government that will have to assume responsibility for carrying out any meaningful urban land policy.

Similarly, while the federal government can and does articulate, along with others, the multiple problems which flow from the local governments, few knowledgeable persons propose that Washington can, or should, attempt to change this institutional setting. To the contrary, local governments are the creatures of the states. The states, in turn, have both the authority and responsibility to review the situation and take steps to modify state-created patterns that no longer respond to the needs of an urban society. Clearly, this is a complex matter, responding to no single, simplistic solution, but there are an assortment of approaches that either significantly ameliorate or go far toward solving the problems which typify this phase of urban life.

Finally, there are other institutional impediments to orderly urban development. High on the list are zoning, building codes, tenant-landlord relations, and local taxation. In these matters, too, the state has the responsibility and the authority to act. So far, only a few states have done so.

What I am saying, to put it bluntly, is that the states do have a vital role in urban affairs, and it is much more than simply becoming another, additional link in the bureaucratic line of administration. If the states want to share in the operation of local programs financed in part by the federal government, they must be prepared to provide financial resources. Rather than concentrating their talents and great leadership potential upon control or additional supervision of such local programs, the states should emphasize developing an assisting and operating role in those urban problems which cannot be performed by local governments and in which the federal government is largely precluded by law and tradition.

VII

There is a universal tendency to seek *the* solution to any and all problems. In a culture which stresses pragmatism to the degree that our does, the yearning for simple and precise answers is especially great. Thus, it is inevitable that the ills of urban America inspire advocacy of simple solutions. The most prevalent one is more and more money, but others are proposed, too, including reorganization of state and local governments, new communities, and abandonment of our existing troubled cities.

With the exception of the latter counsel of despair, there is validity in these and in many other courses of action. However, urban problems are extremely complex and require multiple solutions. Indeed, while it is obvious that a vastly larger amount of money must be made available to urban America, greater federal investment is no assurance of effective action. Money alone will not save our cities or assure orderly development of new areas of urban life.

Three basic ingredients are required if we are to meet the challenge of urbanization. First, more resources are needed. For reasons that are by now well established, this means that the federal government will have to spend more tax dollars in the cities and the surrounding urbanizing areas. The total cost will vary in response to our successes in developing new technology, modifying institutions to permit application of new approaches, increasing and redistributing incomes, learning how to deal effectively with social and human problems, and upgrading the quality of administration.

There are many cost concepts involved. I want to speak of two. The first is the total cost—public and private. The second is public expenditure, involving primarily the federal government but also including state and local governments. Frequently, those who would avoid any sizable public investment in urban America tend to confuse the total cost of meeting our urban requirements with the federal component. A most recent instance of this involved comparison of the estimated cost of an adequate urban future with the cost of the war in Korea and Vietnam. The unsophisticated might erroneously assume that the staggering amount imputed to the former was, like the cost of the wars, public expenditure. This assumption is faulty because it fails to recognize that in housing and urban development and redevelopment, the public investment is but a part of the total outlay. In the larger governmental efforts, private investment greatly exceeds public expenditures. Thus care must be taken to identify each of these two elements in total cost.

Second, we need constantly to develop know-how for dealing with urbanization. Over the past few decades, great progress has been made in identifying the problem areas. We have begun to analyze the costs and conflicts incident to alternative possible solutions. And we are beginning to turn our attention to the institutional impediments that stand in the way of new approaches. Our ability to describe what needs to be done far exceeds our capacity to determine how to do it.

For the tools so effective in getting a man to the moon must undergo great refinement and reorientation if they are to be effective, say, in reducing the cost of housing or facilitating a systems approach to urban development and redevelopment. They must undergo the most sophisticated adaptation if they are to be used in solving complex and cantankerous human problems.

The potential of new scientific approaches to urban

problems is exciting. This method is usually labeled as "systems analysis," and its principal tools and techniques are computers, simulation, modeling, experimentation, and development. The objective is to secure scientific, precise, and comprehensive solutions.

But there are pitfalls as well as great potential. There is no magic in a tool or a sharper instrument of analysis unless it is in the hands of an expert who is sensitive to the limitations of the data and the intricacies of the problems. Computers, systems analysis, and associated machinery and methods are no better than the basic data that are fed into them. Their results can never surpass the viability of the programming and the perception of the programmers. Some have identified this as the GIGO process, namely, garbage in means garbage out.

Even when—and I say "when" advisedly—we do tame the computer, refine the data, and surmount the problems of programming, we shall still have a missing ingredient. That brings me to the third basic need—the need for a cadre of trained people capable of carrying out a broad range of programs and activities.

This is a fairly universal deficiency, involving generalists as well as specialists and including operating personnel at all levels, within government and outside it. Today it is difficult to recruit the talent required to administer our existing programs at their relatively low level of funding. It is inconceivable that we could operate successfully an effort of much greater magnitude without a much larger component of administrators, researchers, operators, and consultants.

VIII

Anyone who speaks of urban America and its problems should do so with humility. This humility reflects a realization of the complexity of the subject. It recognizes that as difficult as are the physical development and rehabilitation of urban America, the human components are vastly more elusive. And it is a bold man who would assert that his pattern for future urbanization represents the optimum.

Yet no articulate citizen can afford not to be concerned. Each should seek constantly to understand better the process of urbanization and the implications of alternative approaches to meet the problems that face us. In meeting the issues, it is important to keep in mind our vast resources and our constant need to learn how best to employ them.

The cities man has created can be molded and guided by man. Our generation has the responsibility and opportunity to channel this activity into constructive and creative directions.